Reading Pictures

Self-Teaching Activities in Art

Lucy Davidson Rosenfeld

J. Weston Walch, Publisher
Portland, Maine

2   3   4   5   6   7   8   9   10

ISBN 0-8251-1887-5

Contents

A Word to Students . . . v

The Elements of Art (continued)

Art with a Message

A Word to Students

You have probably looked at many works of art without really *seeing* them. Perhaps you have noticed whether they are portraits or landscapes or ballet dancers, or whether they are easy to understand or abstract. You may have quickly said which ones you like and which ones you don't. But most likely you have not noticed many, many things about art. Just as with learning to read, the language of art holds a large number of surprises.

That is why we call this book *Reading Pictures*. These exercises are designed to let you discover for yourself what each artist had in mind, and why his or her work looks different from another artist's work. Each exercise will help you to find important characteristics of a work of art, compare it with others of a similar subject, and finally, figure out for yourself what each picture is about. Sometimes you will have the chance to try your own hand at making art, or to describe in your own words what you see. We hope that when you have completed these exercises you will not only look *at* art, but will see what is in it and get new enjoyment from it.

Please remember that these are not competitive exercises. Sometimes there is no "right" answer. Look at these pieces of art and try to "read" what they have to say. Try to capture the aims and mood of each artist. Do not rush through these questions. (In fact, you may find lots of instances where you will want to continue your answers on another sheet of paper.) Refer to the pictures as you answer and try to keep an open mind about each work of art, whether you find it beautiful, strange, or ugly. Enjoy yourself!

Lucy Davidson Rosenfeld

Art As a Reflection of a Civilization

1. *Inca wood carving.* c. 16th century.

2. *German sculpture.* 12th century.

Exercise 1

Jungle Cats: Learning About a Society from Its Art

From the earliest times, art has depicted people's relationship to animals. The pictures you see here are two examples of animals in art. They were made by artists in two different civilizations. By "reading" such pictures carefully, and trying to understand the attitude of the artist toward the subject, you can learn a great deal. You can understand how people of the artist's time and culture depicted the natural world, how they felt about wild animals, and the part animals played in their lives.

1. What are five possible situations in which people might interact with wild animals? (Example: They could look at a wild animal in the zoo.)

   _____

   _____

   _____

   _____

2. How do both of these pictures show "respect" for wild animals?

   _____

   _____

3. In which picture is the jungle cat fiercer?

   _____

4. How can you tell?

   _____

   _____

5. In which is the cat more protective? Or is the cat victorious, having destroyed the man?

   _____

6. A man appears in only one of the pictures, but a human attitude is part of them both. Explain how this is so.

   _____

   _____

7. What characteristics of the animals are exaggerated in each picture?

_____

_____

8. The twelfth-century image appears beside the entrance to a church. Can you think of a reason for placing this statue there?

_____

_____

9. The Inca carving is actually a wooden vase. Why might the artist choose such a fierce image for an everyday item?

_____

_____

10. Which civilization do you think was better acquainted with the natural habitat of the wild animal? Explain your answer.

_____

_____

11. Which picture shows an animal with more "human" characteristics? Which shows the animal more in its natural state? Which is decorated more realistically?

_____

_____

_____

12. Besides wild animals, can you think of some other subjects of art that would help you to understand a civilization? (Example: pictures of their gods.)

_____

_____

_____

13. Choose a twentieth-century country and imagine that you are one of that country's artists. How would you depict a lion or jungle cat? Explain your answer. (You may draw your answer if you prefer.)

_____

_____

_____

Exercise 2

An Egyptian Prince: The Art of Ancient Egypt

In ancient Egypt, paintings filled the tombs of the dead. On the next page is a picture of a prince of Thebes. His tomb was decorated with many scenes showing his activities in daily life, so that he could recreate these happy moments in the afterworld.

1. What are some of the things you can recognize in this tomb painting?

   _____

   _____

2. What are some of the happy or pleasant aspects of this scene that were added to assure the prince's happiness in the afterlife?

   _____

   _____

3. How is the prince depicted? What is unusual about his profile (as in all ancient Egyptian profiles)? Describe the other figure.

   _____

   _____

4. Egyptian art was filled with hieroglyphics (picture writing). What examples can you find? What symbols do you recognize?

   _____

   _____

   _____

5. Egyptian art remained relatively unchanged in style for some 3,000 years. (If you think about Western art over even the last 1,000 years you can see how dramatically art changes over time.) Why do you suppose Egyptian art was so remarkably similar for so long?

   _____

   _____

   _____

"Sennofer, A Prince of Thebes." Egyptian tomb painting. Eighteenth Dynasty.

6. Why do you suppose artists were important people in Egyptian society?

_____

_____

_____

7. How can you tell that the prince is outdoors? (List several ways.)

_____

_____

_____

8. Would you call this style of art realistic? Explain your answer.

_____

_____

_____

9. What are some of the things an archaeologist or historian could learn about life in ancient Egypt from looking at this picture?

_____

_____

_____

_____

10. What details in this picture suggest the Egyptian relationship to and uses for nature?

_____

_____

_____

_____

11. Describe in your own words how this picture would be the same as, or different from, a similar scene of two people in a summer garden today.

_____

_____

_____

_____

Exercise 3

Greek Warship: Ancient Greece, the Geometric Era

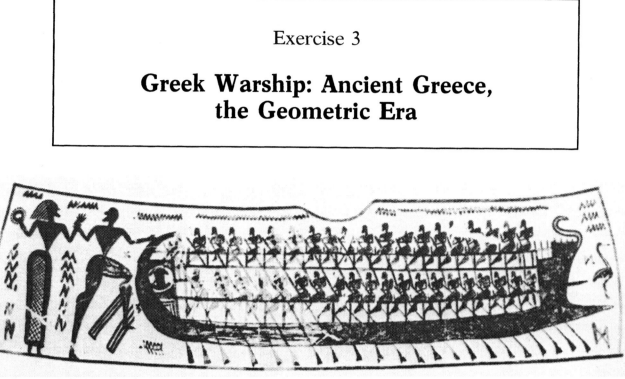

Greek vase painting. 8th century B.C.

Ancient Greek artists painted scenes on vases and other objects. Here you see the decoration of a vase made before the Classical era. Designs such as this one can tell you a great deal about life in this early period, as well as about the artistic taste and style.

1. Describe what you see in this picture. What does the scene show?

_____

_____

_____

_____

2. What are some of the things you can tell about ancient Greek life from this picture?

_____

_____

_____

_____

3. Why would you guess that this early period in Greek art is called "the Geometric era"?

   _____

   _____

4. Note the figures of the man and woman. Why do you think art historians describe this era's art as "stylized"? What shapes are the bodies made up of?

   _____

   _____

5. Aside from the small designs in the empty spaces, what gives this picture its strong design?

   _____

   _____

6. Which lines curve and which are straight?

   _____

7. Which designs repeat many times? Draw them.

8. Can you guess why this design has a long, narrow shape? Why do you think vase painting has lasted longer than much other ancient painting?

   _____

   _____

9. What clues do you have that the man on the left is going off to war?

   _____

10. *Bonus*: How did Greek art change in the Classical era from this early look? What is the difference in how the body is shown?

    _____

    _____

"Kneeling Woman." Baluba sculpture (Congo). 19th–20th century.

Exercise 4

African Sculpture

This highly polished sculpture comes from the Congo area of Africa, where it was made by the Baluba tribe. Like most tribal art, it had both a practical use and a ritual use in tribal ceremonies. African art, which is today prized by museums and collectors, was originally made for ceremonial use by the tribes. Each tribe had its own style of art, but there are some characteristics that are common to most African art.

1. Most African tribes believed that the spirit resided in the head. How can you tell that by this sculpture?

_____

_____

_____

2. The proportions of bodies in African sculpture are very different from those in Western art. Describe the proportions of this body. (Clue: Is the body as large in relation to the head as you expect?)

_____

_____

_____

3. This sculpture was made as a useful object (in addition to its ceremonial use). What do you suppose it was used for?

_____

_____

_____

4. Each part of the sculpture is carved away from a solid mass—probably part of a log. How do you suppose the original shape of the log affected the shape of the sculpture?

_____

_____

_____

5. Most African tribal art is wood sculpture. Why do you suppose African artists used wood more than other substances, such as stone?

_____

_____

_____

6. Most African tribal art is sculpture, rather than painting or other forms of art. Why do you think this is so? (Clue: Keep in mind the isolation, the geography, the climate, and the use of art in tribal Africa.)

_____

_____

_____

7. The Baluba tribe was noted for beautifully crafted, highly polished wooden figures like this one. The skill of the carver was handed down from generation to generation. Why do you suppose artists in primitive tribal societies had very important roles?

_____

_____

_____

8. This figure was not designed to be realistic in the Western sense. In fact, much of its beauty comes from its unusual forms and shapes and spaces. When Western artists in the twentieth century became familiar with African tribal art they were fascinated by it. Some of them imitated it. Why do you think modern artists found African sculpture like this so interesting?

_____

_____

_____

9. Why do you think African art retained the same style from year to year (within each tribe), until the arrival of colonial invaders?

_____

_____

_____

Exercise 5

Medieval People: The Art of the Middle Ages

From the three pictures on the next page, you can tell many things about the Middle Ages. Each of these artworks was made between the eleventh and thirteenth centuries. Each example is fashioned from different (artistic) *media,* or materials. See if you can spot some of the major characteristics of medieval art.

1. Which of these art treasures is made of carved stone? Which is made of bronze? Which is painted?

_____

_____

2. The stone sculpture has a special, quiet quality. How would you describe the woman it represents?

_____

3. The bronze statue has typically medieval proportions. Describe the figure and his horse. How do you know he is going to war?

_____

_____

4. The miniature (painting in a manuscript) shows a violent act. What is it? How do you know the victim is a saint (even without the title)?

_____

5. Which two examples use distorted (or unrealistic) proportions? How does this distortion make the picture more powerful?

_____

_____

6. In the painting, the hands and faces are very prominent. Why?

_____

7. Why do you think the artist painted St. Margarita with her eyes closed, while the murderer has a huge open eye?

_____

1. *"Isabel d'Aragon."* 13th century.

2. *"Medieval Horseman."* 11th or 12th century.

3. *"Martyrdom of St. Margarita."* 12th century.

8. These works of art depict different aspects of religious fervor, which was so important in medieval times. How do these religious messages differ from one another?

_____

_____

_____

9. In which examples do you get a sense of the violence that was also common to the Middle Ages?

_____

_____

10. All of these artworks include many rounded or circular forms. What is the one straight line in the "Martyrdom" that contrasts with the curving lines? What about in the statue of the horseman?

_____

_____

11. Medieval artists were not concerned with the realistic depiction of the human form. In fact, sometimes their art looks almost like abstract art. One way they avoided depicting human anatomy was by covering it up. Find two examples.

_____

_____

12. How would you describe a society that made these three works of art, if all you knew about it was what you see here?

_____

_____

_____

_____

13. *Bonus:* Why do you suppose modern twentieth-century artists were influenced by medieval art as they turned toward abstract art? What did they find in it that they did not see in more realistic art?

_____

_____

_____

_____

1. Master of the stories of Helen. *"The Embarkation of Helen for Cythera."* c. 1445–1470.

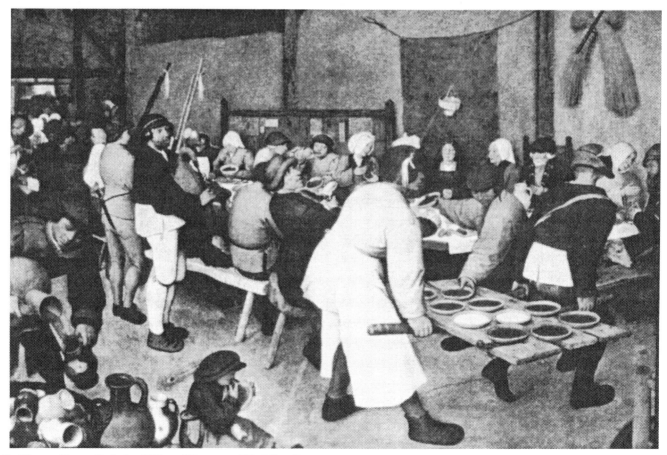

2. Pieter Brueghel the Elder. *"Peasant Wedding."* c. 1565.

Exercise 6

Renaissance People: The Renaissance in North and South

These two paintings were made about 100 years apart. Picture 1 (c. 1445–1470) was made by an Italian artist working during the Renaissance. Picture 2 was made by a Flemish artist in about 1565. By examining these pictures carefully, you can see many differences between Northern and Southern (Italian) Renaissance art.

1. Picture 1 illustrates an ancient Greek story of how the beautiful Helen sailed for the island of Cythera. Describe what you think is happening in the picture.

_____

_____

_____

_____

2. Describe the buildings and rocks and garden. Are they realistically painted?

_____

_____

_____

3. Identify some characteristics that make this painting seem very formal.

_____

_____

_____

4. The dog (at right) is a symbol of faithfulness, while the tiny animal in one woman's hand (an ermine) is a symbol of purity. Why do you suppose the artist included these symbols?

_____

_____

_____

5. Although the story this picture tells took place in ancient Greece, the picture does not try to imitate the look of that period. How can you tell when it was painted? (List at least five ways.)

_____

_____

_____

_____

6. Picture 2 was made by Pieter Brueghel the Elder, a great Flemish artist in northern Europe. His works depicted peasant life and rural landscapes. Describe what you think is happening in this picture.

_____

_____

_____

_____

7. While Italian Renaissance painters focused on classical or religious subjects, what kind of art was popular in the North, judging by this painting?

_____

_____

_____

_____

8. Would you describe picture 2 as more or less formal than picture 1? Explain your answer.

_____

_____

_____

_____

9. How did paintings like the one in picture 2 lend dignity to peasants and their daily life?

_____

_____

_____

10. What details can you spot in this painting that show that this is a peasant wedding banquet, rather than an elaborate dinner for the wealthy?

   _____

   _____

   _____

11. What does the difference in subject matter between these two pictures tell you about the taste in art of each time and place? What reasons can you think of that might account for the difference?

   _____

   _____

   _____

12. What do you think the artist of picture 2 saw in peasant life that he admired?

   _____

   _____

   _____

13. What do you think the artist of picture 1 would have thought of picture 2? Explain your answer.

   _____

   _____

   _____

14. What are some of the things a historian could learn about life in sixteenth-century Europe from picture 2?

   _____

   _____

   _____

   _____

15. Which painting do you like better? Why? Which occasion would you rather be present at? Why?

   _____

   _____

   _____

A Fifteenth-Century Bridal Couple

Jan van Eyck. "*Giovanni Arnolfini and His Bride.*" 1434.

If you learn to look carefully at a painting you may discover many more things of interest in it than at first meet your eye. You can read a painting like a book; this picture, for example, is filled with interesting information. See what you can discover about the couple shown here by answering the following questions.

1. This is a wedding portrait, made in 1434. Describe the couple as carefully as you can.

_____

_____

_____

_____

2. Aside from the obvious difference in clothing, in what ways would you say this marriage portrait is different from a marriage portrait today? How is it similar?

_____

_____

3. How can you tell that the artist wanted to show the couple's social standing or wealth? What details tell you their status?

_____

4. Why do you think he included their furnishings and their full figures?

_____

5. What does the woman's dress and the way she is standing tell you about her? (Keep in mind that large stomachs and small chests and shoulders were in fashion at the time.)

_____

6. What can you guess about the man's character or personality?

_____

7. Why do you think the artist included a mirror on the back wall?

_____

8. There are a number of symbols in addition to the clear details in this painting. Symbols are signs that have familiar meaning. The little dog, for example, represents faithfulness; the burning candle is another symbol. The couple have removed their shoes. Can you guess the meaning of these symbols, and why the artist included them?

_____

_____

9. What is the source of light in this room? How can you tell? (Clue: Look at the shadows.)

_____

10. What do the slanting lines of the window, for example, tell you about the artist's knowledge of perspective? (Explain why these lines slant.)

_____

11. What are some of the different textures the artist has reproduced? How would some of the items in the room feel to the touch? What does the variety of these textures tell you about the artist's technique?

_____

_____

12. Do you like this picture? Why or why not?

_____

Exercise 8

The American Frontier

George Caleb Bingham. *"Raftsmen Playing Cards."* 1847

In the nineteenth century American artists produced an extraordinary collection of paintings depicting the beauties of the American landscape, from the Hudson valley to the Western plains. They were able to combine realistic scenery with a romantic vision. In this painting George Caleb Bingham shows us a scene of river life in the Midwest.

1. Why would you call this painting realistic? Find at least five details that are accurately depicted.

   _____

   _____

2. Do you think the group of men on the raft "happened" to be in the position in which they are shown, or did the artist pose them that way? If so, why?

   _____

   _____

22

3. In what way is this painting like a still life?

_____

_____

_____

4. The light is very important in this work. How can you tell where the sunshine is coming from and what time of day it is? Is the clarity realistic?

_____

_____

_____

5. There is tremendous stillness in this painting. Why does it seem so still?

_____

_____

_____

6. What does this picture say about the beauty, freedom, pleasures, and so on, of the raftsman's life? Do you think this was a realistic view?

_____

_____

_____

_____

7. How does the painting of the raft contrast with the surrounding landscape? Is this a "romantic" vision of raft life? Why or why not? What qualities in a picture might suggest a romantic view?

_____

_____

_____

_____

8. Where is the center point of the picture? (Find the lines of a giant "star" shape that is central to the composition of the painting.) Where does the converging of the important lines of boat and riverbank lead your eye?

_____

_____

_____

9. The grouping of the men contentedly playing cards contrasts with the quiet, uninhabited scenery. What is the artist suggesting about the pleasure of companionship and its relationship to unspoiled new lands?

_____

_____

_____

_____

10. Why do you think Americans, who liked storytelling pictures and landscapes, loved this artist's work? What did it say to them about American values and the beauty of the country?

_____

_____

_____

_____

11. In summary, name some of the ways the artist combined objective, realistic painting with subjective, romantic ideas. Would you say the artist "romanticized" what he saw? Why or why not?

_____

_____

_____

_____

What Is Style?

1. *"Egyptian Warrior."* From the Sixth Dynasty, c. 2300–2160 B.C.

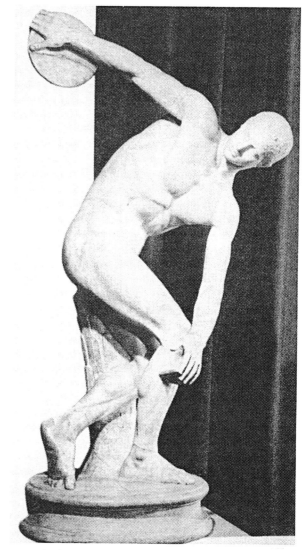

2. *"Discobolus (Discus Thrower)."* (Greek) Roman marble copy after a bronze original of c. 450 B.C. by Greek sculptor Myron.

The Ancient Figure: Egyptian and Greek

These two male figures were made in two very different civilizations of ancient times. There are many differences between them. See if you can identify some of them. For example, how did each artist look at the human body? How did art reflect the ideas of these two ancient cultures?

1. Which statue has the feet and face in profile, but the body facing front? Why does this look strange to us?

_____

_____

2. Which statue shows more concern with the anatomy, the muscles, and the realistic portrayal of the body? Describe the two bodies.

_____

_____

_____

3. Which sculpture gives more of the "idea" of a man rather than a realistic picture of him?

_____

4. Which sculpture has a kind of writing on it that identifies its origin?

_____

5. Which society would you guess cared more about the *beauty* of the human body? Why do you think so?

_____

_____

_____

6. Which society do you think was more interested in proportion and harmony and balance? How does this picture reflect that interest? (Clue: Note the position of the figure.)

_____

_____

7. Which figure shows more strength? More determination? More power? Explain your answer.

_____

_____

_____

_____

8. Why would you guess that this Egyptian style of art stayed the same for over 2,000 years, with only minor changes in how the human body was represented? What can you conclude about a society in which art does not change?

_____

_____

_____

_____

9. While the Greek sculpture looks very realistic when compared to the Egyptian figure, in some ways Classical art is unrealistic. Can you think of a way in which this statue might *not* be true to nature? (Clue: Is the body typical or average?)

_____

_____

_____

_____

10. In what way do these two sculptures represent the difference between two-dimensional and three-dimensional art? (Clue: Could you walk around the Egyptian sculpture and see the back of the figure?)

_____

_____

_____

_____

Three Thoughtful Men

Themes are often universal in art. On the next page are three different works of art with a similar theme: a seated man in contemplation. Yet each piece looks very different. The difference is in their *style*; each artist approached the same subject in an entirely personal way, related to his own culture and time. Try to discover what "style" really means.

1. Which sculpture do you think is the oldest? Why?

   _____

   _____

2. Which do you think is the most recent? Why?

   _____

   _____

3. Describe each work as carefully as you can.

   _____

   _____

   _____

   _____

   _____

   _____

4. What emotion do you think each piece expresses?

   _____

   _____

   _____

5. Which piece is the most realistic?

   _____

6. Which piece is the most emotional?

   _____

1. Nikolaus Gerhaert. *"Portrait Bust."*

2. *Mendi sculpture.*

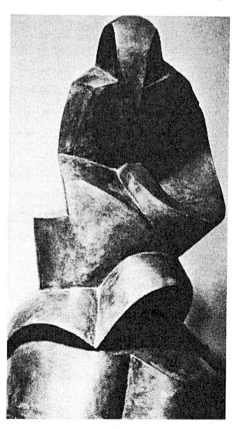

3. Max Weber. *"Spiral Rhythm."*

7. Which piece has the most simplified shape and form?

_____

8. In which piece is the head the most important? Why do you think it was designed that way?

_____

_____

9. If you had to give a new title to each sculpture, what would it be?

_____

_____

_____

10. What is the same about these three sculptures?

_____

_____

11. Look carefully at picture 1. Describe the kind of civilization you think it came from. Do the same for pictures 2 and 3. (Give reasons for your answers.)

_____

_____

_____

_____

_____

12. What do you think "style" means?

_____

_____

13. Make a list of ten words that you think describe each of these sculptures. (Some of the words can be the same for each list.)

1. _____ _____ _____ _____ _____

_____ _____ _____ _____ _____

2. _____ _____ _____ _____ _____

_____ _____ _____ _____ _____

3. _____ _____ _____ _____ _____

_____ _____ _____ _____ _____

1. Henry Moore. *"Family Group."*
1945–49. Bronze cast, 1950.

2. Alberto Giacometti. *"La Clairière."* 1950.

Exercise 11

Modern Sculpture and the Human Body

The human body has always been a major subject for sculptors. From the block statues of the ancient Egyptians to today's contemporary works, sculpture of the human shape has taken numerous forms. With the twentieth century's emphasis on personal expression rather than strict realism, sculptors have looked at the body in new ways and with different aims and interests.

1. Describe Henry Moore's sculpture. What does it remind you of?

_____

_____

2. Describe the Giacometti work and what it suggests to you.

_____

_____

3. What aspect of the human body seems to most interest the sculptor of picture 1?

_____

4. Why do you think the sculptor of picture 2 made nine figures together? What does their coexistence suggest?

_____

_____

5. Which work is more concerned with convex and concave form? Explain your answer.

_____

_____

6. Which artist would you guess wants to express the isolation of people from their environment? Explain your answer.

_____

_____

_____

7. How has the sculptor of picture 1 modified the way human bodies really look? What has he exaggerated or distorted? What has he left out?

_____

_____

_____

_____

8. What does the simplified form of the bodies in picture 1 suggest about the "family" he sculpted? Are they individuals? Explain your answer.

_____

_____

_____

9. How does the thinness of the figures in picture 2 express the artist's view of humanity? Why do you guess he made the bodies so tall and thin?

_____

_____

_____

_____

10. Which work is smoother in texture (to the touch)? Which has a rougher surface? Why is each texture appropriate for the artist's idea of the human body?

_____

_____

_____

11. Why would you guess that modern sculptors do not simply portray the human body the way it looks in real life? (Both sculptors whose work is seen here made realistic works in their early days.)

_____

_____

_____

12. What do sculptures like this make you think of? On another sheet of paper, write a paragraph or two describing the kind of people you imagine when you look at one of these pictures. Describe their relationships to the other figures in the work.

Exercise 12

Looking at Landscape

1. Meindert Hobbema. *"The Avenue, Middelharnis."* 1689.

Perhaps the most common subject for painting throughout history has been the landscape. Here and on the next page are three very different examples of landscape art; see if you can identify the various aims of each artist, and how each picture treats a tree-filled, rural scene.

1. Which painting has a clear sense of perspective, including a distant spot on the horizon (a vanishing point) from which the lines of the road and

   ground radiate? _____

2. Which landscape treats the shapes of trees and hills like giant pieces of

   sculpture? _____

3. Which painting is composed of numerous small patterns or ornamental designs? Which other painting(s) use repeated designs?

   _____

   _____

2. Raoul Dufy. *"View of Taormina."* c. 1922–23.

3. Grant Wood. *"Young Corn."* 1931.

4. Which painting(s) focus on the three-dimensional form of the trees?

_____

_____

5. Which painting treats the trees in the most realistic way? Explain.

_____

_____

_____

6. Which painter sees the landscape in the most decorative, least structural

way? Explain. _____

_____

_____

7. Each painting uses line in a different way. In picture 1, what do the
lines of the tree trunks and the rutted road indicate? In picture 2, line is
used for a different purpose. How would you describe it? In picture 3,
what do the various kinds of lines indicate?

_____

_____

_____

_____

8. There are people in two of these landscapes. How do they help the
artist make his point about space and distance?

_____

_____

_____

9. There are dark accents in each painting. Which are true shadows?
Which are simply decorative devices (to make the design interesting and
rhythmic) and do not relate to where the sun is shining?

_____

_____

_____

_____

10. In each painting there is a house or building. How important is each house and how does it influence your impression of the landscape around it?

_____

_____

_____

11. Which painting do you like best? Why?

_____

_____

_____

12. In the space provided, draw a landscape of your own. It should include five of the following items: a field, hill, mountain, house, tree(s), river, roadway, tower, fence. (Do not copy one of these landscape paintings.)

Exercise 13

The Beauty of Japanese Landscape

Japanese woodcut prints are among the most admired compositions in all of art history. Western artists such as Degas and Toulouse-Lautrec were influenced by their design. The print on the next page was even copied by Van Gogh. An exhibition of prints like these was so admired when it came to Paris in the late nineteenth century that many artists tried their hands at making them. Hiroshige (1797–1858) was one of the best-known artists of his time.

1. Describe what you see in this picture.

   _____

   _____

   _____

   _____

2. How many horizontal sections is the print divided into? What are they?

   _____

   _____

   _____

3. In the box, draw the major horizontal areas. Leave out the people and the complicated bridge construction. Shade in the darkest areas.

4. What makes the composition seem to balance? Are the horizontal areas completely straight across? Are they all the same in width and size?

_____

_____

Ando Hiroshige. *"Ohashi Bridge and Atake in a Sudden Shower."*

5. How can you tell it is raining in the picture? How do the rain lines contrast with the major areas of the picture?

_____

_____

_____

6. There are some completely straight horizontal lines in the picture. Find several of them and tell what they are.

_____

_____

_____

7. Can you see the "end" of any of the areas in this picture? For example, can you find the end of the bridge, or the last mountain in the distance? How does the artist make you feel as if you are seeing a snapshot of a scene rather than the whole thing?

_____

_____

_____

8. What are the strongest accents in the picture? Why do you suppose these particular areas are the darkest?

_____

_____

_____

9. What curving lines and what straight lines are contrasted?

_____

10. Why do you think this zigzag composition balances so well?

_____

_____

_____

11. *Bonus*: What kind of mood does this picture put you in? Explain your answer.

_____

_____

_____

1. Pieter de Hooch. *"The Bedroom."* c. 1660.

2. *Scroll painting.* 17th century. Japan.

Exercise 14

Paintings of Rooms

The interiors of houses and rooms have been popular subjects with artists for centuries. Here are two examples. On the top is a seventeenth-century Dutch painting showing a bedroom in a comfortable house. On the bottom is a section of a Japanese scroll painting from about the same time. In comparing these two pictures you can discover some differences and some similarities between Eastern and Western art.

1. Both of these pictures show a room with people in it. What is the major difference? Where would the artist have been standing to have seen the rooms from these two angles?

   _____

   _____

   _____

2. The Japanese painting and the Dutch painting do not both use *perspective*. How can you tell what is in the distance, or outdoors, in the Dutch painting? Which lines help show distance? (Clue: Look at the tile floor.)

   _____

   _____

3. In the Japanese painting you can see a great deal more of both inside and outside the house. How can you tell what is inside and what is outside without perspective and windows?

   _____

   _____

   _____

4. The landscape can be seen in both paintings. In which painting does the landscape have more importance? What is its function when seen through the window? In which picture is the landscape more important in its own right?

   _____

   _____

   _____

5. One painting is filled with geometric divisions (mostly rectangles). The other has many more curving and free-shaped areas. Which is which? Find eight rectangles in the more geometric picture and name them (e.g., windowpane).

_____

_____

_____

_____

_____

_____

6. Japanese art is known for its design—both its overall structure and its small ornamented patterns. Find five examples of interesting patterns in the Japanese picture. (Don't forget the outdoor part.)

_____

_____

_____

7. What kind of ornamentation can be found in the Dutch painting? (Clue: Note the chair backs.)

_____

_____

_____

8. In which painting is the light more important? In which is dramatic contrast provided by the light?

_____

_____

_____

9. Which painting focuses more on the people in the room? Describe what you think is happening in each picture.

_____

_____

_____

_____

10. *Bonus*: On another sheet of paper, write a short (one- or two-page) story using one of these two pictures as the subject.

Exercise 15

Looking at Portraits

Faces can be painted in many different ways. There are as many kinds of portraits as there are artists. If you look at the three pictures of old men with beards on the next page, you will see that each artist had different aims.

1. The Renaissance portrait of an old man (picture 1) is filled with realistic detail. What are some of the things you know about the man from this picture?

   _____

   _____

2. Do you think this is probably a good likeness of him? What do you think the artist's aims were in painting him?

   _____

   _____

3. Realistic portrait painting has continued up to the present day. But the invention of the camera in the nineteenth century has had an effect. What would you guess portrait photography's effect on painting has been?

   _____

   _____

4. In the seventeenth-century Korean ink picture (2), another bearded man is shown. What is your impression of this man's personality and appearance?

   _____

   _____

   _____

5. How does the artist's style dramatically emphasize the character of the man? _____

   _____

6. How would you say that picture 2 differs from picture 1?

   _____

   _____

1. Marcantonio Bassetti. *"Old Man with Gloves."* 16th–17th century.

2. Kim Myong-guk. *"Dharma."* 17th century.

3. Jacques Villon. *"Portrait of the Artist's Father."* 1924.

7. Picture 3 is by a French *cubist* painter; it was done in 1924. What characteristics of his father's head seem to have been most important to the artist?

_____

_____

_____

8. What can you tell about the subject's looks and character?

_____

_____

_____

9. How is the artist's twentieth-century interest in pure form expressed?

_____

_____

_____

10. If you compare these three portraits, you can actually see major differences in the aims of artists in different times and places. What would you say were the different objectives of each of these three artists in making these paintings? Which do you like best? Why?

_____

_____

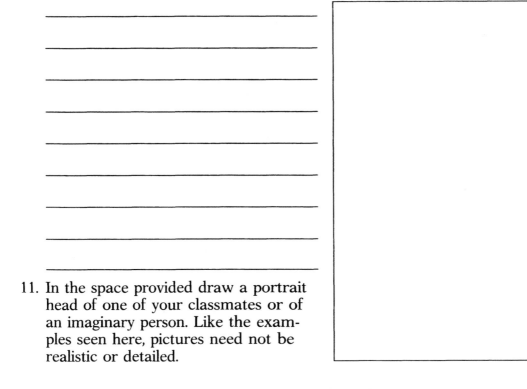

11. In the space provided draw a portrait head of one of your classmates or of an imaginary person. Like the examples seen here, pictures need not be realistic or detailed.

Impressionism

Berthe Morisot. *"In the Dining Room."* 1886.

In the late nineteenth century in France, a group of painters founded a new style of painting called *Impressionism*. They were attempting to capture an "impression" in paint of a particular moment. Their emphasis was on the quality of light and its effect on the colors and shapes of the scene. Berthe Morisot, who painted "In the Dining Room," was the first woman artist to join the Impressionist group.

1. How does the artist's style of painting express the idea that the maid was not posed in this way, but "caught" as she passed by?

   _____

   _____

2. What details in the painting show that she was in the middle of her

   work? _____

   _____

3. In what ways does the painting resemble a photographic snapshot? (Clue: Notice the borders of the picture.)

   _____

   _____

4. What are two ways that you can tell where the light is coming from?

   _____

   _____

5. How does the artist show that this is not just a portrait of a person, but a total scene? What would be different about the picture if it were a portrait only?

   _____

   _____

6. How can you tell that the cupboard door is made of glass?

   _____

7. Why is the floor darker in front of the figure?

   _____

8. In what ways would you guess the subject matter of this painting differed from traditional subjects for paintings of the time?

   _____

   _____

9. One critic of the Impressionists remarked about Morisot: "She is interesting to behold. In her, feminine grace is preserved amidst the frenzy of a mind in delirium." Why do you guess Impressionism seemed "frenzied" to critics of the time?

   _____

   _____

10. Do you like this style of painting? Why or why not?

   _____

What Is an Abstraction?

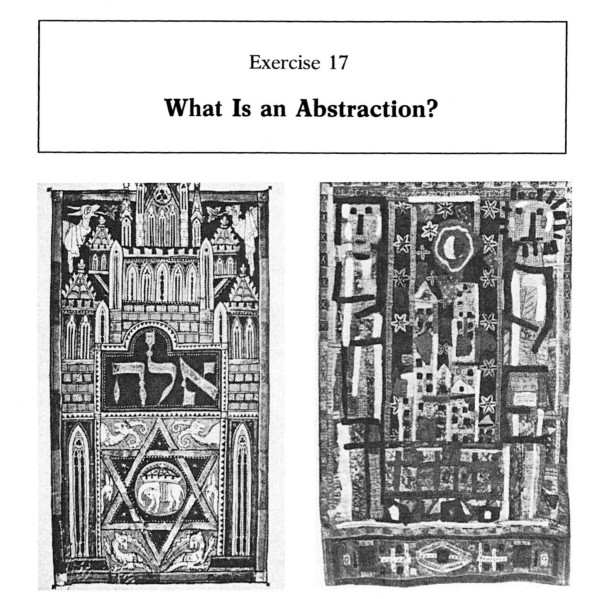

1. *13th-century Hebrew frontispiece from a Bible.*

2. Roger Bissière. *"Cathedral."* 1946.

These two paintings were made more than 700 years apart. They have many similarities and some important differences. If you can answer the following questions, you may better understand *abstract* painting.

1. Describe picture 1 as carefully as you can.

_____

_____

2. Describe picture 2.

_____

_____

_____

3. What kind of shapes does each painting consist of?

_____

_____

_____

4. Is anything behind anything else in either painting? Is there space or distance?

_____

_____

_____

5. What are some of the recognizable objects in picture 1? What do you think they symbolize?

_____

_____

_____

6. What are some of the recognizable objects in picture 2? What do you think they symbolize?

_____

_____

_____

7. In the diagrams below make a rough outline of the major design of each picture.

8. What did you discover about the design of each picture? (Clue: Are they symmetrical—matching one side to the other?)

_____

_____

_____

9. The medieval artist of the Hebrew Bible used a complicated and beautiful design to express his message. The contemporary artist used a similar design, but had no biblical message included in his painting. What do you think is the meaning of the word "abstraction" in regard to painting?

_____

_____

_____

10. What were the artists' different aims?

_____

_____

11. How would you define an abstraction or abstract painting?

_____

_____

_____

The Elements
of Art

1. Ambrogio Lorenzetti. *"View of a City."*

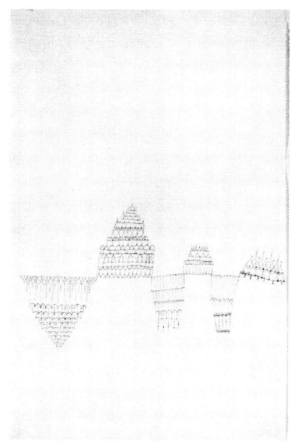

2. Paul Klee. *"Pagodas on Water."* 1927.

3. Robert Delaunay. *"Eiffel Tower."* 1924–1926.

The Artist's Point of View

By "point of view" we mean both "where you are standing to get a view of something" and "what your attitude is." Artists have to decide what view of their subject they wish to depict, what they want to emphasize, and what attitude they want to take toward their subject. These three pictures all show towers or tall buildings. But each artist had an entirely different point of view.

1. Picture 1 is by a Renaissance artist named Ambrogio Lorenzetti. It is a view of a city. Describe the scene, including as many details you can.

   _____

   _____

   _____

2. Where do you suppose the artist was standing when he sketched this picture? Below the city? Above it? To one side?

   _____

3. What appears to be his major interest in showing this city? (Clue: Why are there no people in the scene?)

   _____

   _____

4. Picture 2 is by the twentieth-century Swiss artist Paul Klee. Describe what this picture shows. (Clue: Note the title).

   _____

   _____

5. What was the artist's point of view—where might he have been standing to make this picture? Was he near or far away? Why do you suppose there is no background included?

   _____

   _____

6. Why do you think some of the pagodas or towers are upside down?

   _____

   _____

7. Though the artist probably imagined this view, he had a very clear point of view. What would you guess was his major interest in showing this scene?

_____

_____

8. Picture 3 is by a French painter named Robert Delaunay. Where would the artist have been standing to see this view of the tower?

_____

_____

9. What seems to have interested him the most about the construction of the tower? What did he find interesting about the ground around it?

_____

_____

10. In what ways would you say this picture is realistic? In what ways abstract?

_____

_____

_____

11. In the empty boxes below, draw a tower or tall building three times. In each box draw it from a different point of view: up close, from a distance, in detail, inside, outside, and so on. Caption each picture carefully.

Exercise 19

Formal Compositions

Some paintings, particularly during the Renaissance, were made with a specific geometric structure or composition. Each of the three paintings you see on the next page has such a design as the basis for its composition.

1. What is the major structure of the columns and walls in picture 1? Draw it in the frame provided here.

2. Why do you suppose this is an appropriate structure for a Christian theme?

_____

_____

_____

_____

3. What part of the picture is most important in your opinion—the architecture or the figures?

_____

_____

4. In picture 2, what is the major shape? (Don't forget the hills on either side of the picture.)

_____

_____

5. Draw the shape in the frame provided here.

1. Piero della Francesca. *"The Annunciation."* c. 1452–1466.

2. Giovanni di Paolo. *"Descent from the Cross."* c. 1426.

3. Neri di Bicci. *"The Coronation of the Virgin."* Mid-15th century.

6. How do the figures fit into the design structure? Draw a line on your sketch in question 5 that shows how your eye moves from the figure at the far right across the picture to the figure at the far left.

   _____

7. Why do you suppose there are two tiny people at the bottom front of the painting?

   _____

   _____

   _____

8. In picture 3, what is the major shape? Draw it in the frame provided here.

9. What are some of the reasons the artist might have thought that this shape was a good idea for the subject of his picture (God crowning the Virgin Mary)? Keep in mind that the painting was made before Columbus's journey to America.

   _____

   _____

   _____

   _____

   _____

10. In the frame provided here, choose a familiar shape and design a picture around it. (Example: cone, triangle, circle, etc.)

What Is Symmetry?

1. *Dutch tile design.* Early 17th century.

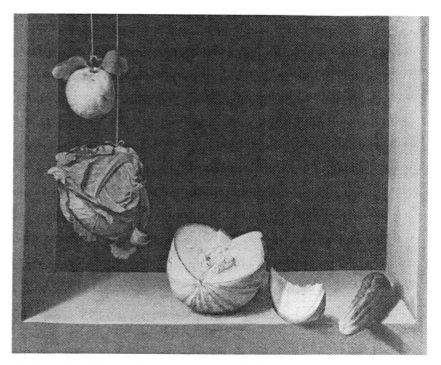

2. Juan Sanchez Cotán. *"Quince, Cabbage, Melon and Cucumber."* c. 1602.

Do you know what *symmetry* or *symmetrical* means? Symmetry is the basis for design in thousands of different kinds of art. See if you can discover some things about symmetry and its opposite, *asymmetry*.

1. Which of these two pictures matches one side to the other, almost exactly? Which is symmetrical, or equally balanced?

_____

_____

2. Which picture is asymmetrical, so that the balance is not equal from one side to the other?

_____

3. Which picture looks more decorative, like the designs you see on wallpaper, pottery, or fabric?

_____

4. Which picture's design moves your eye from one direction to another? Put an arrow on each picture that indicates which way your eyes move when you look at it.

_____

5. In which picture do you see the design as a whole unit, and in which do you look first at one thing and then at the next? Explain your answer.

_____

_____

6. Why do you suppose the artist of picture 2 hung two objects on strings?

_____

_____

7. What would you suppose is the relationship between the different fruits and vegetables in picture 2? (Clue: Note that some of the fruit is cut and opened, some whole, and that they have different shapes.)

_____

_____

8. What symmetrical objects can you see in your classroom? (Clue: Look for a clock, a vase, etc.)

_____

9. Which kind of balance—symmetry or asymmetry—is more peaceful to look at? More interesting? More disturbing? Which do you prefer? Explain your answer.

_____

_____

10. In the two boxes below, draw four balls or other objects of your choosing, like fruit, bottles, or flowers. In box 1 set them in a symmetrical pattern (but not exactly like the Dutch tile design). In box 2 set your four objects in an asymmetrical pattern so that they do not balance evenly (but not exactly like the still life).

Box 1   Box 2

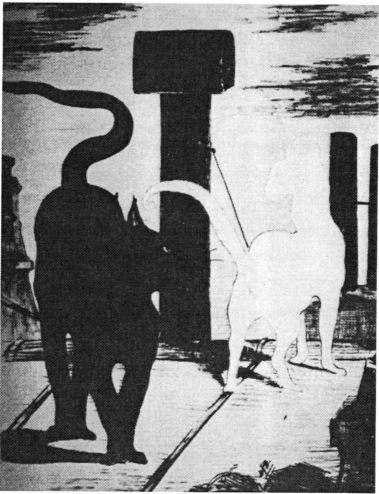

1. Edouard Manet. *"Cats on the Roof."* 1868.

2. M.C. Escher. *"Encounter."*

3. Victor Vasarely. *"Bhopal."*

Exercise 21

Black-and-White Design

1. What do all of these pictures have in common?

_____

_____

2. What are the major black areas in picture 1, "Cats on the Roof"?

_____

3. What are the major white areas in the same picture?

_____

4. Are they of equal importance?

_____

_____

5. Which lines are curved; which are straight? Why do the two cats stand

out? _____

_____

6. In picture 2, describe what you see.

_____

_____

7. Which are the major black-and-white areas in picture 2? Explain fully.

_____

_____

8. Which is more important—the black design or the white design? Explain
your opinion.

_____

_____

9. Is there "negative" or empty space in this picture? Why or why not?

_____

_____

10. In picture 3, which areas—black or white—seem more important? Explain.

_____

_____

_____

11. If you said you thought they were equal in importance, why do you suppose that is?

_____

_____

12. Would you say there is empty space in this picture? If so, where is it?

_____

13. What are the major contrasts in this picture? (Look at shapes, sizes, etc.)

_____

_____

14. What makes strong black-and-white designs interesting?

_____

_____

15. Photocopy the forms below, cut them out, and on another sheet of paper, arrange them in a design (either realistic or abstract) so that they make a unified, interesting, balanced, and strong black-and-white picture. (You need not use all of the shapes, and you may add lines if you wish.)

Exercise 22

Mary Cassatt and the Design of a Painting

Mary Cassatt. *"The Boating Party."* 1893–94.

This is one of the American artist Mary Cassatt's most famous and beloved paintings. It reflected a number of new ideas in 1893 when it was made. See if you can spot these new ideas.

1. In what way is this picture like a snapshot, instead of a posed picture?

_____

_____

2. What gives it a sense of motion?

_____

_____

3. Impressionists believed in capturing the moment's impression. How does the design of this painting emphasize that idea?

_____

_____

_____

4. Why do you have the impression that you are sitting in the rear of the boat?

_____

_____

5. In what ways is this a realistic picture? Describe what is taking place.

_____

_____

_____

6. In what ways does it seem quite abstract or unrealistic?

_____

_____

_____

7. What would you guess about the woman's social position? Explain your answer.

_____

_____

_____

8. Cassatt almost always chose to paint mothers and children. Why would you guess they were her favorite subject?

_____

_____

_____

9. Why do you think Cassatt's Impressionist-style paintings were poorly received in America, but accepted in Europe? What would be some reasons that Americans disliked her style of painting?

_____

_____

_____

10. Two of the major influences on Cassatt were Japanese woodcut prints and the works of Edgar Degas. Both the prints and Degas' works explored asymmetrical, balanced design. In the box below, draw a big "X" dividing the space into quarters. (This will help you figure out what goes where.) Now draw in the major areas of the picture, such as the rounded outline of the boat, the oars, the sail, the horizon line, and the people.

11. Find the wide-edged triangle that is an important part of the design. Outline it.

12. Find the major diagonal "thrust" that cuts the picture in two. Draw it.

13. Blacken in the darkest area and outline the lightest.

14. Describe the design of the diagram you have made. Why do you think later abstract artists were so interested in this painting?

_____

_____

_____

_____

15. Do you like this painting? Why or why not?

_____

_____

_____

_____

_____

1. One-dimensional *embroidered dragon*.
Early Ch'ing Dynasty, 17th century.

2. Two-dimensional *tile dragon*.
Ming Dynasty, 1368–1644.

3. Three-dimensional *pottery dragon*.
Ch'ing Dynasty, 1644–1911.

Exercise 23

One, Two, and Three Dimensions: Three Chinese Dragons

The dragon is an important symbol in Chinese art. It appears in many different ways: in weaving, pottery, sculpture, painting, embroidery, and carvings. The three dragons you see here represent only a few of the different types of dragons found in Chinese art, for some are fierce, some are playful, and some are good-luck symbols. These three dragons will help explain the differences between one-, two-, and three-dimensional art.

1. Picture 1 shows a dragon embroidered on a cloth robe. You can see the front of the dragon clearly, but can you see its sides? Its back?

   _____

2. What makes it appear round if it is really a flat piece of embroidery?

   _____

   _____

3. Is picture 1 more like a painting or a sculpture? Does it have volume?

   _____

4. Picture 2 is a dragon from a wall in the Forbidden City in Beijing. It is made of ceramic tile. If you touched it, do you think you could feel any roundness to it?

   _____

5. Is the dragon in picture 2 as flat as the dragon in picture 1? _____

6. Is there a back to the dragon in picture 2? Could you walk around it and see it from the back? If the tile is attached to the wall, what would you see if you walked around it? Does the tile have a rounded shape in both front and back?

   _____

   _____

7. Picture 2 is a form of sculpture called *relief* sculpture, often used to decorate walls. It has some roundness, but it is not fully round. It is called two-dimensional. How can you tell this particular dragon is a sea dragon?

   _____

8. The dragon in picture 3 is a pottery sculpture. Does it have a front, sides, and a back?

   _____

9. Now that you have seen three different kinds of Chinese dragons, what are some of the similarities in their design? Describe each one.

   _____

   _____

   _____

10. What kind of lines or forms are most evident? (Clue: Chinese art has very few straight, angular lines.)

    _____

    _____

11. Chinese art is filled with symbols, such as flames. Can you find any symbols that appear in these pictures? Can you guess what they might represent?

    _____

    _____

    _____

12. Which dragon do you find scariest? Does the fact that it is one-, two-, or three-dimensional have anything to do with your answer? Explain.

    _____

    _____

    _____

13. In the following list, underline the kinds of art that are three-dimensional. Circle the kinds of art that are one-dimensional. Put a checkmark over the art that is two-dimensional.

    painting   relief sculptures

    embroidery   weaving

    drawing   mobiles

    miniature carving   prints (etchings)

    objects glued to a wall or collage   sculpture

    posters   photographs

Exercise 24

Showing Volume

The human body has volume, or mass. It is composed of a series of three-dimensional, rounded forms. Artists have used many different means to express the shapes of the human body. While sculptors can work with rounded, three-dimensional forms themselves, painters have to find other ways to show volume. The three pictures on the next page portray the human body in very different manners. See if you can identify these methods.

1. Which picture uses the most anatomical detail? Describe it.

   _____

   _____

2. Which picture depends on dark-edged abstract shapes to show the forms of the body? Describe it.

   _____

   _____

3. Which pictures use many lines to express the volume of the body? Describe them.

   _____

   _____

4. What kinds of lines are they? How do they accentuate the roundness of the body?

   _____

   _____

5. Which pictures use shadows to accent the volume of the body? Point out the places where you see shadows.

   _____

   _____

6. Which picture would you guess was made in medieval times, when the study of the human body was not considered important?

   _____

1. *"St. Mark,"* from *Gospel Book of Archbishop Ebbo of Reims.*

2. Michelangelo. *"The Last Judgment,"* detail of the Sistine Chapel ceiling.

3. Fernand Léger. *"Nude on a Red Background."*

7. Which picture would you guess was made in the twentieth century, when the idea of abstract form was more important than realism?

_____

8. Which picture would you guess was made by an artist who thought the human body was beautiful and should be realistically represented?

_____

9. How does light help show volume in each picture? Can you tell where the light comes from? (Clue: Look at the shadows to find the *source* of light.)

_____

_____

_____

_____

_____

_____

10. In each of the three boxes below, draw a large ball. Show its volume by each of the methods you have just discussed. In box 1, show the ball's volume by using line. In box 2, show the ball's volume by using light and shadow. In box 3, show the ball's volume by darkening the edges and lightening the center.

"Icon of St. George." 14th century.

The Importance of Shape

Icons were movable religious pictures, often painted on wood. They were particularly common in medieval Russia. This example was made in the fourteenth century; it illustrates the well-known story of how St. George killed a dragon. It is also an excellent example of how important shapes can be in the design of a work of art.

1. All of the forms in this icon are outlined with a thin black line. Find the following shapes and outline them on the complete picture. Put the correct number on each one.

2. What kinds of shapes are these? Describe them. (Clue: Are they geometric, like cubes and circles? What do they remind you of?)

_____

_____

3. Find the biggest "X" shape in this picture. Draw it on the picture. (Clue: Look at the spear of St. George and the horse's back.)

4. Look carefully at the frame. What is strange about the relationship of this picture to its frame? How does the frame seem to push the horse and rider out of the picture towards you?

_____

_____

5. There are many curves in this picture. Each one is "balanced" by another curve that looks almost like its opposite. Find three such patterns. (Clue: Look at the "U" shape of the dragon and the horse's neck.)

_____

_____

6. Where do you suppose the artist had to stand to make this picture? Above the scene? Below it? How can you tell? (Clue: Note where the horse and rider are looking.)

_____

_____

7. Where is the dragon in relationship to the horse and rider? What does this tell you about the artist's view of the saint and the dragon?

_____

_____

8. Why is the empty space below the horse's belly (which divides the painting) important?

_____

_____

9. In what ways are the horse's shape and the dragon's shape similar? How are they different?

_____

_____

_____

10. Find two circle shapes, one white and the other black, that contrast with one another. (Clue: Look for the cave.)

_____

_____

11. In the box below, draw six interesting shapes that touch each other and fill up all the space. Do not make any two exactly the same shape or size. Shade some of them.

1. Shigenobu. *"Three Women Dyeing Cloth."*

2. *Acoma Indian pottery design.*

Pattern As Design

In some art, *patterns*—dark and light, straight lines and curves, or a variety of decorative shapes—make up the design. This is true of both realistic and abstract art.

1. In picture 1, what do the straight lines represent?

_____

_____

2. How many different patterns can you find on the costumes of the women? Draw some of them in the boxes provided.

3. What is the major difference between these designs and the lines indicating the window, floor, walls, and chair legs?

_____

_____

_____

4. Name three kinds of contrast you can find in this picture. (Clue: Look at the kinds of lines, shapes, and darks/lights.)

_____

_____

_____

5. In the boxes below, draw some of the patterns you see in picture 2, the American Indian pottery design.

6. How would you describe these patterns in words? How do they differ from one another?

_____

_____

7. In the diagrams above, blacken in the darkest areas and some important lines.

8. What makes your eyes move around these pictures rather than focus on one particular spot?

_____

_____

_____

9. *Symmetry* occurs when parts of the picture are evenly balanced or match one another, so that if there is an accent or strong note in one corner there will be one in the opposite corner. Would you call these pictures *symmetrical*? Why or why not?

_____

_____

_____

10. Are patterns only used in realistic art? Do they have to have a subject, such as flowers or birds or stars?

_____

_____

11. Look at the clothes you are wearing. How many different patterns can you identify on yourself? (Don't forget socks, the soles of your shoes, the knit pattern of your sweater, the designs of fabric, and so on.)

_____

_____

_____

12. On another sheet of paper, make a picture that includes one of the following: six different flower patterns, six different geometric patterns, six different kinds of stripes. Add six black accents so that the patterns are well spaced and not all the same size or shape.

1. *Chinese tile.*

2. *Japanese woodblock print.*

Exercise 27

Motifs or Repeated Patterns

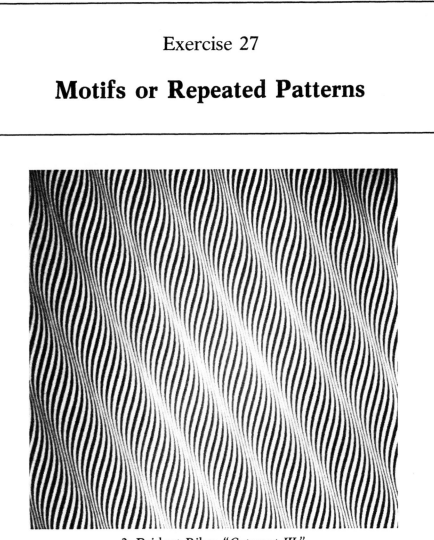

3. Bridget Riley. *"Cataract III."*

Artists often use a repeated pattern to represent familiar sights such as the water currents shown in these three pictures. They do not give you a realistic picture of each wave and ripple. Instead they use a stylized form of design, called a *motif*. When the motif is repeated many times you recognize it and understand its meaning. The three examples shown here are from different eras and different cultures; picture 1 from Ming Dynasty China (1368–1644), picture 2 from Edo-era Japan (1615–1868), and picture 3 from modern Great Britain (1967). See if you can identify the motifs and what each artist wanted to express about the movement of water.

1. In box 1 on the next page, draw a typical wave shape as you see it in the Chinese tile. In box 2, draw a wave the way it appears in the Japanese woodblock print. In box 3, draw the pattern that Riley used.

2. How can you tell that the wave pattern in the Chinese tile represents water?

_____

_____

Box 1

Box 2

Box 3

Box 4

3. Is the water shown on this tile a quiet body of water, or a rough ocean? How can you tell?

_____

_____

4. The Japanese print pattern is more complicated. What is happening to the ship?

_____

_____

5. What kind of lines did the artist use to show the force of the current? Describe fully.

_____

_____

6. What method did the artist use to show that the waves were coming from many different directions at once? How did he accentuate those directions?

_____

_____

7. In the third picture, by contemporary artist Bridget Riley, what kind of lines suggest the current of a waterfall? Describe fully.

_____

_____

8. Why do you suppose this kind of art is called "op"or optical art? (What does it make your eyes do?)

_____

_____

9. In box 4, design your own pattern that could be repeated over and over in a picture to represent falling rain or snow.

10. Repeated patterns create a kind of rhythm, just as they do in songs or poetry. Can you think of an example in music or poetry in which the same images or words are repeated again and again? Write it below.

_____

_____

_____

_____

_____

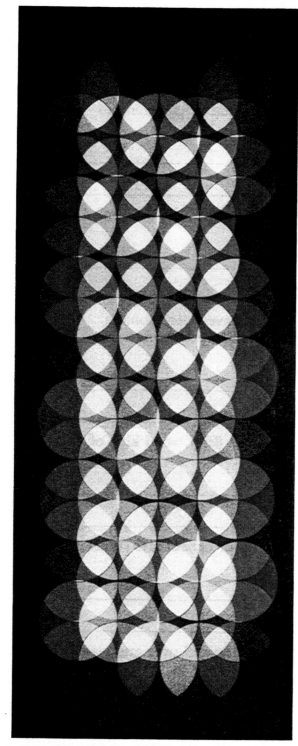

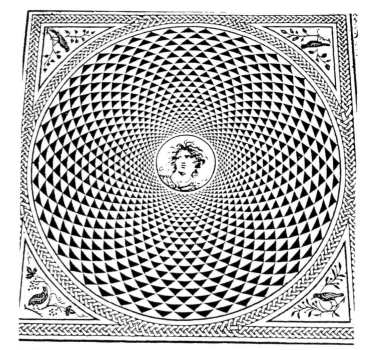

2. *Roman mosaic.* First century A.D.

1. Francisco Sobrino. *"Unstable Displacement."* 1968.

3. *Op Art design.*

Exercise 28

Optical Illusions and Op Art

Here are three different examples of optical-illusion art (Op Art). These are pictures that change as you look at them. They have deceptive patterns that alter your perception as you see them. Optical illusions were popular in art as far back as ancient Rome. One of the major periods of optical art is much more recent: the 1960's and 1970's. See what you can discover about Op Art by answering the following questions.

1. Picture 1, by Francisco Sobrino, is made of Plexiglas. It has dozens of small intersecting circles. Name some of the ways you think the artist makes your perception of the small circles change. (Mention light and dark patterns, intersecting lines, and so on.)

   _____

   _____

   _____

   _____

2. Picture 2, the Roman mosaic, is circular. Stare at it for a moment. What do you see? A disappearing round hole with a face in the distance? A series of circular waves pushing the face to the front? Which way do the arcs or waves of triangles move? Describe what you see.

   _____

   _____

   _____

   _____

3. How is this optical illusion in picture 2 created? (Mention the sizes of the triangles, their shapes, the kind of lines used, and where the larger shapes are in relation to the smaller ones.)

   _____

   _____

   _____

   _____

   _____

4. Picture 3 is a design made up of two hexagons (six-sided shapes) that are related. There are two major centers. Which goes backwards, which comes forward? Can you tell? Describe why you think one recedes and the other emerges. (Clue: What is the importance of the lines that radiate from the center of each hexagon?)

_____

_____

_____

5. In the diagram below, draw a continuation of this same design. How would it repeat?

6. How would you guess that the Roman mosaic was made at an earlier time than the other two examples shown?

_____

_____

7. The diagrams below and on the next page show you some examples of simple optical illusions. Complete each drawing as directed.

   a. Make this drawing into the roofs of three houses.

b. Make this drawing into three boxes.

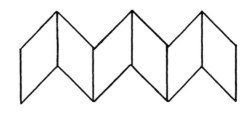

c. Make the first drawing into two faces looking at one another.

d. Make the other drawing into a wine glass with straws and fruit on top.

8. What do these exercises tell you about optical illusions? Can you think of any other optical illusions?

_____

_____

_____

9. Op Art usually has no subject, such as a landscape or still life. It is usually geometric in design. Do you think it is interesting or boring art? Explain why.

_____

_____

_____

_____

Dramatic Lighting

Artemisia Gentileschi. *"Judith and Maidservant with the Head of Holofernes."* c. 1625.

The use of light in a painting can be as dramatic as stage lighting. By the seventeenth century, dramatic lighting with brilliant clarity and deep shadows had become very important in painting. This work by a well-known woman artist in Italy is a good example of how lighting affects the drama of a painting.

1. This biblical scene shows Judith, the standing figure, who has just cut off the head of the invading general, Holofernes, in order to save her city. Describe what you think is happening at the moment captured in the painting.

_____

_____

2. Why are the strong contrasts of dark and light particularly suitable for the subject of this picture?

_____

3. What is the source of the light? _____

4. How can you tell? _____

5. How does the strong ray of light make you aware that this is a diagonal composition, with the most important forms in the painting placed from

   top left to lower right? _____

_____

5. How is this lighting exaggerated? Why do you suppose the artist chose to make the contrast so strong?

_____

_____

6. Where are you as a viewer while this action is taking place? Close or far away? What effect does the closeness of the action have on you? Would you see the lighted action this clearly if it were farther away?

_____

7. What does this dramatic picture tell you about styles in art at the time? What kinds of themes, emotions, and treatment of subjects were popular, judging by this picture?

_____

_____

_____

8. Which parts of the painting has the artist lighted most clearly, and which are most in shadow?

_____

_____

9. When does a theater producer use the kind of dramatic lighting shown here? What kinds of scenes are lighted in this stunning way?

_____

_____

10. *Bonus:* Why do you suppose this was a very controversial painting when it was first presented by the woman artist, Artemisia Gentileschi?

_____

_____

Exercise 30

Dramatic Art: The Use of Contrast

A dramatic moment is captured in this painting by American artist Everett Shinn. How did the artist make his picture so exciting? See if you can discover a number of strong contrasts that emphasize the dramatic event.

1. What is the lightest area in the picture? What is the source of the light?

   _____

2. What are the darkest areas? (Don't forget to look at the acrobat himself.)

   _____

3. What are the most curved areas?

   _____

4. What are the straightest areas?

   _____

5. What does the contrast between the curving and straight lines emphasize?

   _____

   _____

6. Where are the smoothest textured areas? The roughest?

   _____

   _____

7. How do they affect the story? (Clue: When he hits the ground, will it be soft or hard?)

   _____

   _____

8. What do the two sections of broken rope tell you about the story? What do they accentuate in the painting?

   _____

   _____

9. How does the figure of the acrobat's partner (the woman in the background) contrast with his falling figure?

   _____

   _____

10. Why do you think all of these contrasts make the picture more dramatic?

    _____

    _____

11. On another sheet of paper, write a short (several paragraphs) story that might accompany this picture.

1. *"Nahkt and His Wife."* Egyptian tomb painting, Eighteenth Dynasty. 1557–1304 B.C.

2. Li T'ang. *"Two Sages."* 12th century.

3. Pierre Auguste Renoir. *"Oarsmen at Chatou."* 1879.

Exercise 31

Distance and Space

Eastern and Western artists have shown distance or space in landscape painting in different ways throughout history. The three pictures you see here all include several figures standing beside a body of water. In each one the landscape, and in particular the area behind the water, is shown differently, as is the relationship of the figures to the scenery. Understanding how artists treat distance or space is an important clue to understanding the art you see.

1. How did the Egyptian artist show that the pond had four sides? Is there any distance or distant scenery?

2. Why are some of the trees upside down in the Egyptian painting? Where would you have to be standing to get a view like this?

3. In Li T'ang's painting the distance is much greater. Can you find the end of it? Why or why not?

4. What method does the Chinese artist use to show that distance and space are infinite?

5. In the Impressionist painting by Renoir, what indicates the limits of the lake? How can you tell its size?

6. How does Renoir show you that things across the lake are smaller than those nearby? Explain.

_____

_____

_____

7. In which pictures are the figures the most important? Least important?

_____

_____

8. In which picture would you say the natural beauty of the landscape has more importance than the figures? How can you tell?

_____

_____

9. In which pictures are there a distinct foreground (front area), middle ground, and background?

_____

_____

10. Which artists show that distance blurs clear outlines? Explain.

_____

_____

_____

11. Which artist shows that forms placed one behind another suggest distance or space? Explain.

_____

_____

_____

12. Which painting uses diagonal lines in a zigzag pattern to suggest distance across the water?

_____

13. In the box on the following page, draw a free-form body of water, such as a lake. See if you can add landscape details, such as trees or houses, so that the distance across the lake is indicated clearly. Do not make an overhead view (like that seen from an airplane).

The Importance of Line

Théodore Géricault. *"Frightened Horse."*

This drawing of a frightened horse was made by a French artist who worked in the Romantic style. By using *line* in a variety of interesting ways in this dramatic drawing, the artist was able to show that the horse was moving excitedly.

1. What particular parts of the horse give you a feeling of movement?

   _____

   _____

2. What do the darker lines, such as those in the center of his body, emphasize?

   _____

   _____

3. How can you tell that the horse has bulk or mass? Are there any straight lines?

_____

_____

4. How do the horse's tail and mane contrast with each other?

_____

_____

5. There are many extra lines in this drawing—extra in the sense that they do not specifically show the outlines of the horse itself. Do you think they add anything? If so, what?

_____

_____

6. How does the more delicate drawing of the horse's head add to the feeling of fright?

_____

7. In contrast, how does the rougher drawing of his hind legs and tail add to the feeling of the horse's fright?

_____

8. Would this be as exciting a picture if it were neater and had no blots? Why or why not?

_____

_____

9. In what ways do you think drawing can be a particularly good medium for showing a dramatic incident like this? What can a drawing do that other kinds of art cannot? (Clue: Imagine a sculpture of a frightened horse.)

_____

_____

_____

10. *Bonus:* Dramatic, exciting pictures of nature were typical of Géricault's era. This artist was in the forefront of the Romantic movement in art. Can you think of any ways in which this drawing could be called romantic? (Clue: Would a carefully drawn horse grazing beside a fence be just as "romantic"?)

_____

_____

1. Vincent van Gogh.
"The Washerwomen." 1888.

2. Wassily Kandinsky. *"Improvisation 28 (Second Version)."* 1912.

Both paintings and drawings have many lines. Often these lines are used to create a feeling of movement and excitement. Line is one of the most important elements of art, whether it is a long, stretching outline or a short fragment.

1. What is happening in van Gogh's drawing? Describe the scene. (Clue: Notice the title.)

_____

_____

_____

2. What is Kandinsky's painting a picture of? Does it have a subject? Describe it.

_____

_____

_____

3. In van Gogh's drawing you can see a variety of short lines. Describe four different types of lines he used.

_____

_____

4. What does each one represent?

_____

_____

5. How can you tell that the river is fast-flowing?

_____

6. Which longer lines lead your eye from the foreground to the background?

_____

7. Which lines contrast with other lines in their darkness or direction?

_____

8. In the painting by Kandinsky, how might the lines indicate that it is a landscape? Do any lines suggest landscape shapes? Which ones?

_____

_____

_____

9. Describe some of the things you think the lines represent.

_____

_____

_____

10. If you do not see the painting as a landscape, but as a pure abstraction (a picture of shapes, colors, forms, and lines), what do the lines add to the picture?

_____

_____

_____

11. How do lines in both pictures add excitement and interest?

_____

_____

_____

12. See how many types of lines you can find in each picture and draw them below. (Don't forget to notice which are darker or heavier.)

13. The word "rhythm" is usually used in music. How can it also describe lines in art?

_____

_____

_____

Exercise 34

Texture: Three Faces

Texture refers to the sense of touch, or how something feels. In art, different media have different textures. The texture of a work of art is a very important part of how the work looks to you. The same image made of heavy, thick globs of paint would seem very different if it were woven in a silky strip of cloth. The three faces shown on the next page have strikingly different textures.

1. Which picture do you think is made of small bits put together to make a whole?

   _____

2. Is the face rough or smooth looking? How did the artist vary the lights and darks to show the different features?

   _____

   _____

3. Why would this type of art be appropriate for wall decoration?

   _____

   _____

4. Which picture is the most realistic in terms of shape and modeling? Why? (Clue: What medium do you think the artist used?)

   _____

   _____

5. What does the texture of the face—the thin, parallel lines—accentuate about the face? (Clue: Note their direction.)

   _____

   _____

6. What is the difference in the use of lines between pictures 1 and 2? Do the lines in each face go the same way?

   _____

   _____

   _____

1. *Mosaic.* 12th century.

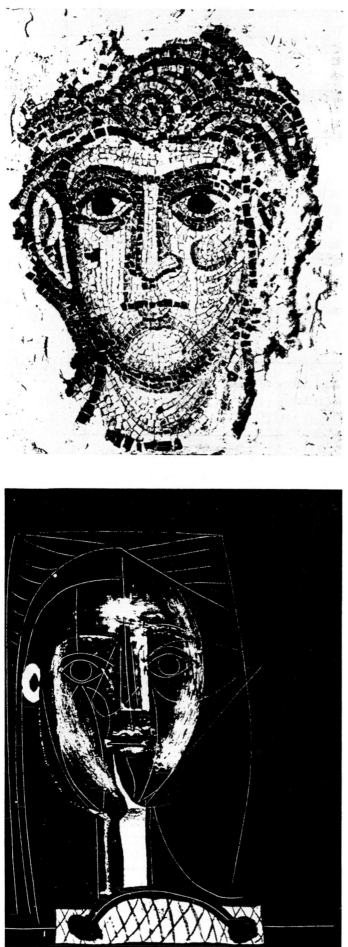

2. *Bronze portrait head,* from Ife, Nigeria. 12th century.

3. Pablo Picasso. *"Black Head."*

7. Which of the two faces would you describe as three-dimensional (having a front, sides, and back)?

_____

8. Picture 3 uses texture in a different way. How many kinds of white lines or textures can you count? Draw arrows to them from the margin.

_____

_____

9. What do the scratchy white areas on the cheeks add to the picture?

_____

_____

10. How does this picture suggest that the face might move, or turn in a different direction? How are the possibilities for a different view of the face indicated?

_____

_____

_____

11. What artistic textures and media can you think of that are (a) smooth? (b) Rough? What would you use to best show (c) a head of curly hair? (d) A silky gown? (e) A sticky patch of wet tar? (f) The chrome bumper of a new car? (g) A beach filled with pebbles? (h) A shadowy figure on a dark, moonless street?

a. _____

b. _____

c. _____

d. _____

e. _____

f. _____

g. _____

h. _____

Mixed Media

Marisol (Escobar). *"Poor Family 2."*

This is a very large contemporary work by the Venezuelan artist, Marisol Escobar. She uses a variety of materials to make an artistic and social statement.

1. What different materials can you spot in this picture?

_____

_____

_____

_____

2. Describe this work as carefully as you can.

_____

_____

_____

3. Why do you think the artist used these particular materials for the house? Explain.

_____

_____

4. What are the people made of? How do they express the artist's feeling about them? Why do you think they are placed where they are?

_____

_____

5. Describe the door and the doorway.

_____

_____

6. Works like this include "found" objects—things picked up on the street or in a junkyard. How do these elements add to this piece of art? Which parts do you think the artist found and reused?

_____

_____

_____

7. How do the woman's hands add feeling to this work?

_____

8. What are some of the different jobs that the artist did in making this work? How does this labor parallel the lives of the poor family in the work?

_____

_____

9. This kind of work is a construction in mixed media. Do you think it would be as interesting or strong in another medium, such as a painting or drawing? Explain why or why not.

_____

_____

10. On another sheet of paper, write a very short story based on this work of art.

Collage

1. Robert Rauschenberg. *"Dam."* 1959.

2. Romare Bearden.
   "The Intimacy of Water." 1973.

Both of these works were made by pasting together various kinds of material such as paper or cloth. This technique is called *collage*; it is a popular art form in the twentieth century.

1. Picture 1 is called "Dam." How does the artist give the idea of a dam in this seemingly abstract or unrealistic picture?

_____

_____

_____

2. What does the pasted-on printed material suggest?

_____

3. Why did he allow this material to look decayed or crumbling, particularly at the bottom?

_____

_____

4. What are many dams covered with? What makes their surfaces change?

_____

_____

5. What does the mixture of different kinds of surfaces suggest?

_____

_____

6. What is the subject of picture 2?

_____

_____

7. How did the artist's use of collage help him to make the water seem varied and realistic?

_____

_____

8. What quality of the ocean and shoreline does the collage capture very well?

_____

9. How do the two figures in picture 2 relate to the water around them?

_____

_____

10. How is accident or chance used in this kind of art?

_____

_____

11. Can you think of any other type of art in which chance plays a role? (What about music?)

_____

12. Choose one of these two pictures and, on another sheet of paper, write a short story of several paragraphs that captures the atmosphere of the picture.

1. Pablo Picasso. *"The Bullfight."* 1934.

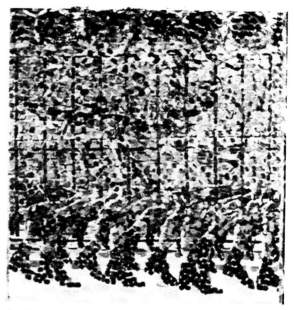

2. Giacomo Balla. *"Girl Running on a Balcony."* 1912.

3. Jacob Lawrence. *"Runners."* An Olympic poster. 1972.

Showing Motion

In the twentieth century artists have used a variety of ways to show motion or action. Instead of simply representing a body in the position of movement, they have tried to show motion or movement itself.

1. Describe what is happening in each picture.

   _____

   _____

2. What are some of the ways that Picasso has emphasized the action of a bullfight? Be specific in your answer.

   _____

   _____

3. How does the jumble of lines suggest exciting action?

   _____

   _____

4. How does the artist show you that an action-packed event is not seen as individual, separate movements, but as an overall spectacle of movement?

   _____

   _____

5. In picture 2 the artist, Giacomo Balla, wanted to show a girl running. What method did this Italian artist use?

   _____

6. What other kind of medium or art form uses many tiny images shown one after another?

   _____

7. Why is repetition important in picture 2?

   _____

   _____

8. Why do you suppose this kind of art was called "Futurism"?

_____

_____

9. How can you tell that Balla's girl is running on a balcony?

_____

_____

10. In picture 3 the black American artist Jacob Lawrence depicted five Olympic runners. How does his depiction of their bodies emphasize motion? Be specific in your answer.

_____

_____

11. How does the striped, curving track accentuate their movement?

_____

_____

12. How does the different size of each runner add to the sense of motion?

_____

_____

13. Which picture most clearly captures a sense of motion, in your opinion?

_____

14. Choose one of these three pictures and list twenty words that describe its action.

_____   _____

_____   _____

_____   _____

_____   _____

_____   _____

_____   _____

_____   _____

_____   _____

_____   _____

_____   _____

Art with a Message

Exercise 38

Ritual Art: Navajo Sand Painting

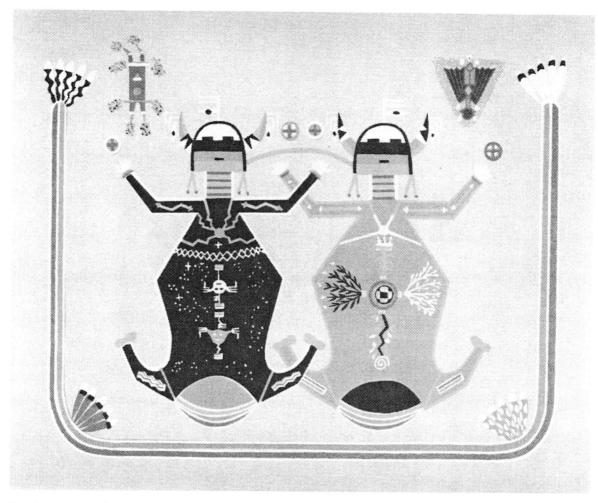

"Father Sky and Mother Earth." Navajo sand painting.

Among the most interesting art of American Indian tribes is sand painting. Here is an example of Navajo art. This picture was made as part of a ceremonial ritual for curing the sick. A complete sand painting can require dozens of artists working all day.

1. Describe Father Sky (on the left) and Mother Earth (on the right) as carefully as you can.

   _____

   _____

   _____

2. What symbols (pictures of familiar things) can you recognize?

   _____

3. There are growing plants on Mother Earth's body. Why would you guess they are there?

   _____

4. Why do you suppose Father Sky is dark and has white spots?

   _____

5. The large three-sided arc around the two bodies represents the rainbow goddess. What do you suppose her empty hands (at each end of the design) are used for?

   _____

6. What can you tell about the Navajo attitude toward nature from this picture?

   _____

   _____

7. Why would this sort of art be called *symbolic* (filled with symbols)?

   _____

   _____

8. Why do you think non-Indian settlers had little appreciation for Indian art?

   _____

9. Why do you suppose sand painters are so important to their cultures?

   _____

10. Why do you think this picture was used for a ceremony for curing sick people? What does it tell you about the Navajo attitude about illness?

    _____

    _____

    _____

11. Why do you suppose the colors in sand painting are almost entirely tans, dark reds, and other earth tones?

    _____

12. What other kinds of art might be part of Navajo ceremonies? (Clue: Would people stand quietly during the ceremony?)

    _____

    _____

Symbols in Art

Baugin. *"The Five Senses."* c. 1630.

A still life is a collection of objects arranged by the artist into a design that interests him or her. In some still lifes the objects themselves have a symbolic meaning, so that the canvas has both an artistic and thematic message. See if you can discover some of the ideas of the artist who made this painting.

1. There are a number of objects in the painting. Can you identify them?

   a. a round, cut-open loaf of bread

   b. an octagonal mirror

   c. _____

   d. _____

   e. _____

   f. _____

   g. _____

   h. _____

   i. _____

2. Many of these objects are symbols (pictorial signs) of the five senses. Can you name the five senses, and tell which object represents which sense?

   _____

   _____

   _____

3. There are many diagonal lines or thrusts in the painting. They help to move your eye from the front of the painting toward the back. What are some of these lines?

   _____

   _____

   _____

4. In addition to the diagonals, the artist combines many contrasting shapes and textures. See if you can identify the different shapes of the objects and how they would feel if you touched them.

   _____

   _____

   _____

5. What two items jut out into "your" space—out of the picture's interior? What do you think this technique accomplishes?

   _____

   _____

   _____

6. This painting is a kind of riddle, because the artist makes you guess what it means. What do you think it "means"? There are several possible answers. (Clue: Don't forget the bag of money, the playing cards, and the chessboard, as well as the symbols of the five senses.)

   _____

   _____

   _____

7. Now that you have examined this picture carefully, what do you think a symbol in art is?

   _____

   _____

8. On another sheet of paper, write a short story that this picture might illustrate.

1. Jan Steen. *"The Eve of St. Nicholas."* c. 1660–65.

2. Doris Lee. *"Thanksgiving."* 1935.

These two paintings were made about 300 years apart, but they have much in common: Both are *genre paintings*. See if you can discover what genre painting is by answering the following questions.

1. Both paintings show a large family preparing for a holiday. Pick one painting and describe fully what you see and what you think is happening.

   _____

   _____

   _____

2. In each painting the room in which the families are seen is very important to the meaning of the picture. Describe each room and the kind of family that is busy within it.

   _____

   _____

   _____

3. What important lines in each painting give the dimensions of the room and indicate the perspective? Explain.

   _____

   _____

4. What mood is expressed in each painting? What clues are there to this mood?

   _____

   _____

5. Each painting presents a certain set of values or an overall impression. In picture 1, St. Nicholas has just visited the family and left toys for all the children except one. Explain what you think the painting says about the manners or values of its time.

   _____

   _____

6. In painting 2, which was made in the 1930's, the artist also presents a picture of the ways or manners of a certain time and place. What kind of American life-style is the artist portraying?

_____

_____

7. When a museum acquired this painting, there was quite a battle between those favoring more contemporary styles of art and supporters of this type of work. Why do you suppose more conservative viewers loved this painting?

_____

_____

8. Think about our modern life-style. Give two reasons that you suppose genre painting, like these examples, is less popular now than in the past. What has changed?

_____

_____

9. Would you say there is any relationship between genre painting and short stories or anecdotes? What is it?

_____

_____

10. What media today depict family life and domestic scenes that were the subjects of genre paintings in the past? Explain your answer.

_____

_____

_____

11. Explain what you think genre painting is.

_____

_____

_____

12. Choose one of the two paintings and, on another sheet of paper, write a very short story about what happens at the holiday celebration shown. Use the painting as your guide to characters and setting.

Art with a Moral

The picture on the next page tells a story with a moral. The artist has given us many clues to understand what is happening. Answer the following questions and see if you can figure it out.

1. Where is the miser?

   _____

2. Who are some of the people or creatures in his room? (Find and describe five of them.)

   _____

   _____

   _____

3. Give two ways that you can tell the miser is dying. Which figure represents death?

   _____

   _____

4. Where does the miser keep his riches?

   _____

5. Two major figures are fighting over the miser. Who are they? Describe them.

   _____

6. Symbols are signs that represent ideas. This picture has many symbols that represent good and evil. Find several of each and describe them.

   _____

   _____

   _____

7. The miser has to make a choice before he dies. What do you think this choice is?

   _____

8. Why does the man leaning over the treasure chest carry both a key and a rosary (a symbol of Christian prayer)?

   _____

Hieronymus Bosch.
"Death and the Miser." c. 1490.

9. What are the devil and angel doing?

_____

10. What course do you think the miser will take? Why?

_____

11. What does this picture tell you about the artist's view of greed, wealth, religion, and human nature? Write your answer on another sheet of paper.

12. On another sheet of paper, write a very short story about this miser and why he suddenly finds himself in this terrible predicament.

Exercise 42

The Artist As Revolutionary

Artists have played a special role throughout history as social critics and sometimes revolutionaries. With their art they have focused on injustice and incited people to rise up against their governments. In many times and places their works have been banned and they have been persecuted and jailed for their views. On the other hand, many governments have used artists to further their policies and make propaganda by glorifying the government's successes through art. For the most part, however, artists have been critical of their governments, exposing injustices and fomenting change.

1. George Grosz is making a strong social point in his picture on the next page. Explain what is happening.

_____

2. What does the title mean? _____

3. What does this artist think of a society that puts its poor out in the

   snow? _____

4. What strong symbolism does he use? Explain it.

_____

5. Siqueiros was a Mexican artist who believed that his country's policies were destroying the common people. How can you tell that he identified himself with the workers?

_____

6. Why do you think he made his fist bigger than his face in this self-portrait?

_____

7. What is he saying about the artist's power to effect change?

_____

_____

8. His arm breaks through the picture's space, toward the viewer. What does this composition suggest?

_____

_____

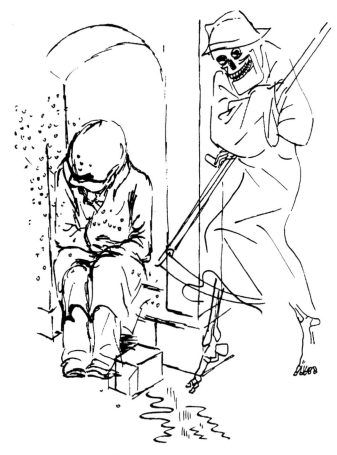

1. George Grosz. *"Eviction."* 1935.

2. David Alfaro Siqueiros. *"Self-Portrait."* 1943.

9. Describe how each artist uses symbolism or distortion to make his point.

_____

_____

_____

10. In the box provided or on another sheet of paper, use one of these two methods (symbolism or distortion) to show a viewpoint of your own. Give the picture a title. (Do not copy these pictures; make up your own "cause." Examples: ecology, prison reform, drug use.)

Exercise 43

Art As Satire

Thomas Rowlandson. *"The Chamber of Genius."* 1812.

The Englishman Thomas Rowlandson was one of the best-known satirical artists. His works conveyed to the public his views about society's habits and weaknesses. With clever drawing and accurate details, Rowlandson made a great impression as an artist and social critic. See if you can identify some of the techniques of the satirical artist.

1. The title of this work is "The Chamber of Genius." What is the meaning of this title?

   _____

2. How many rooms does the artist live in with his family? What does the family consist of?

   _____

3. What is the subject of the painting by the "genius"?

   _____

   _____

4. Describe what is going on around the artist while he paints.

   _____

   _____

5. Find three items in the picture that refer to other kinds of "genius" than painting.

   _____

6. What details tell you that the artist is poor? And sloppy?

   _____

   _____

7. What do you think Rowlandson is making fun of? The genius who wishes to live in such disorder? The society that allows its geniuses to live this way? The genius's wife? Explain your answer.

   _____

   _____

   _____

8. The quotation under the picture reads: "Want is the Scorn of every wealthy Fool. And Genius in Rags is turn'd to Ridicule." (The meaning of the word *want* is "poverty.") What do you think this quotation means in relation to the picture?

   _____

   _____

9. The artist has used exaggeration, symbolism, and overcrowding to emphasize his point. Give examples of each device.

   _____

   _____

10. In spite of these exaggerations, would you call this realistic art? Explain your answer.

    _____

    _____

11. Why do you suppose satirical art like this amuses some people, angers others, and is often repressed by governments? Is it art that is simply meant to be beautiful? Explain your answer.

    _____

    _____

    _____

Pop Art

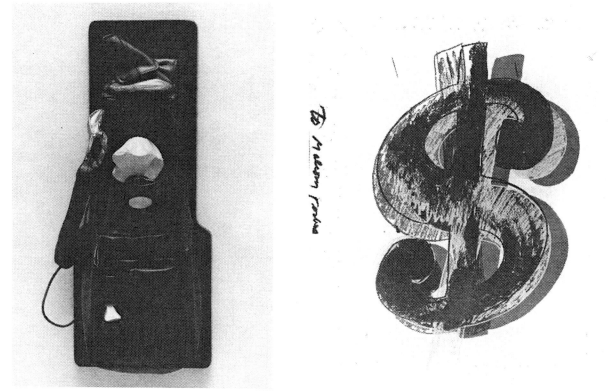

1. Claes Oldenburg.
   "Soft Pay-Telephone." 1963.

2. Andy Warhol. *"Dollar Sign."* 1980.

In the 1950's a new style of art called Pop Art developed in London, and then the United States. Pop Art combined the techniques of advertising, film close-ups, and packaging with familiar objects of mass culture. Some Pop Art was based on comic strips, some on advertising images such as billboards and commercials. Some Pop artists took well-known pictures or images and blew them up into giant paintings; others repeated one image over and over. Two examples of Pop Art are shown here. See if you can discover some characteristics of Pop Art.

1. One of the most well-known Pop artists was Andy Warhol, who made the "Dollar Sign" you see here. Why do you think the dollar sign is so big in relation to the size of the picture?

_____

_____

_____

2. How does this picture relate to advertising?

_____

_____

3. Do you see a message in this picture? In your opinion, is this a humorous or satirical picture?

_____

_____

_____

4. Oldenburg's "Soft Pay-Telephone" is made of vinyl filled with stuffing. What does the choice of a soft substance to portray what is normally a hard, shiny object tell you about the artist's idea for the work?

_____

_____

5. Describe the work as fully as you can.

_____

_____

_____

6. Is there a message in this work, or do you think it is simply a humorous idea?

_____

_____

7. Do you see any relationship between these two pieces of art? If so, what is it?

_____

_____

_____

8. Both of these pieces are single images, not surrounded by background as in more traditional art. How do these examples of Pop Art relate to the images we see daily on television, on billboards, in movies, and so on?

_____

_____

_____

9. Why do you suppose Pop Art was the cause of controversy in the art world? What would more traditional artists feel was missing from it?

_____

_____

_____

10. Choose a familiar item and draw it in the box below in a Pop Art style. Below your picture explain why you think you have made an example of Pop Art.

_____

_____

_____

_____

Exercise 45

Dreams and Surrealism

For centuries artists have made pictures of imaginary events. One of the great possibilities of art is that it can make the imaginary seem real. The two pictures on the next page are examples of dream images by well-known artists.

1. Describe what is happening in picture 1, "The Nightmare."

_____

_____

2. Are the grinning cat and the ghostly horse really visiting the woman? How does the artist answer that question?

_____

3. What means has the artist used to make you believe this is an actual event?

_____

4. How does this combination of real and unreal suggest dreams? Describe a dream of your own that *seemed* real, but was not possible.

_____

_____

_____

5. In the Romantic age, the late eighteenth-century artist often depicted exotic or dramatic subjects, and many works involved dreamlike images. Can you guess some reasons why?

_____

6. Describe what you see in picture 2, "The Therapeutist."

_____

_____

7. In what century would you guess that this work was made? Explain.

_____

8. Is this work realistic? Explain how.

_____

1. John Henry Fuseli. *"The Nightmare."* 1785–90.

2. René Magritte. *"The Therapeutist."*

9. How does the artist combine what is possible with what is not?

_____

_____

10. What profession do the cape, the bird cage, and the hat suggest to you? Why do you think the artist chose those particular items?

_____

11. The title of picture 1 suggests what is happening. What do you think the title "The Therapeutist" (meaning one who helps the sick or unhappy) signifies?

_____

12. Magritte (the artist who made picture 2) is called a "surrealist." After reviewing your answers to questions 8 and 9, explain what you think *surrealism* is.

_____

_____

_____

13. In the box below, draw a picture of a dream or imaginary event. Give it a title that helps explain it.

Exercise 46

A Personal View of History

1. Horace Pippin. "*John Brown Going to His Hanging.*" 1942.

This painting, called "John Brown Going to His Hanging," is by Horace Pippin, a black American artist. The scene shows John Brown, the white antislavery rebel, who was hanged on December 2, 1859, just before the beginning of the Civil War. Pippin based his painting on his mother's description, and he gives a personal view of the historical event.

1. Describe what is happening in the painting.

   _____

   _____

2. How can you recognize the jail that Brown was kept in?

   _____

3. Which figure represents John Brown, and how can you tell?

   _____

4. How can you tell what season of the year it is?

   _____

   _____

5. What is the significance of the coffin that Brown is sitting on?

   _____

   _____

6. How would you describe the crowd? Why are two figures on the right turning away from the sight?

   _____

   _____

   _____

7. What other ways has the artist used to express grief? (Clue: Mention trees, the use of black and stark white, etc.)

   _____

   _____

8. How does the close-up view accentuate the drama of the scene?

   _____

9. How does the design of the painting call attention to the figure of John Brown?

   _____

10. What do you think the artist meant when he said about his work, "Pictures just come to my mind and I tell my heart to go ahead."

    _____

    _____

11. What might be the emotions of the different people seen in this picture? (Mention those on the wagon, the crowd, etc.)

    _____

    _____

    _____

12. In what way might this be called a "personal" view of history?

    _____

13. Choose a particular person in this picture and, on another sheet of paper, write a short paragraph, imagining his or her thoughts as the scene occurred.

Exercise 47

How the Artist Tells a Story: Brueghel

Pieter Brueghel the Elder. *"The Blind Leading the Blind."* 1568.

Pieter Brueghel the Elder was one of the greatest painters of the sixteenth century. He used a variety of techniques to make his beautiful paintings tell a story to his viewers. See if you can understand the moral of the story, and how the artist managed to tell it.

1. The six figures in this painting are all blind. In what direction are they

   moving? _____

2. How can you tell? What lines lead your eye in the direction that the figures are moving? What lines help accentuate the diagonal and downhill thrust of the picture?

   _____

   _____

3. How can you tell that all the men will fall? (Clue: Note the position of each figure, and the folds of his clothing.)

   _____

   _____

4. Describe the landscape around them. How does it contrast with their descent into the ditch?

_____

_____

_____

5. If you look closely, you will see that this picture is constructed in a geometric design. Its shape is a horizontal rectangle, divided by a diagonal. Outline the diagonal thrust of the picture.

6. Each man will soon fall. What are the different ways in which each one leads another to his fate?

_____

_____

_____

7. What do the different facial expressions tell you about each of the blind men? Describe two of them, indicating which one you are writing about.

_____

_____

_____

8. Brueghel and other artists of his time often included a moral in their works. What moral do you think the artist had in mind here? (Clue: Think about being handicapped, and being a follower.)

_____

_____

_____

9. Would you describe this painting as realistic? Why or why not?

_____

_____

10. What would you say are the characteristics of "narrative" art, or art that tells a story like this one?

_____

_____

11. *Bonus:* Choose a famous saying, such as "haste makes waste" or "the sky is the limit" or "time and tide wait for no man," and, on another sheet of paper, draw a sketch that illustrates the saying. Be sure to put the title on your drawing.

Exercise 48

How the Artist Tells a Story: Curry

John Steuart Curry. *"Tornado Over Kansas."* 1929.

1. What life-style do you think these people had?

   _____

   _____

2. Can you guess where the artist grew up?

   _____

3. Why do you think the artist was known as a "regional" painter?

   _____

4. Is this scene dramatic? What methods did the artist use to show the drama of the situation? (Clue: Mention the lighting, the positions of the people, the scenery, and so on.)

_____

_____

5. Is this a realistic painting? Is there exaggeration, too? Explain your

answer. _____

_____

6. How do the major lines of the picture add to the excitement?

_____

_____

7. Why do you think Curry was known as a particularly "American"

painter? _____

_____

8. What can you tell about the artist's attitude toward farm life, nature's violence, the family, and animals?

_____

_____

9. How can you tell the date of this picture?

_____

10. In an era when American art was frequently dominated by French and other European styles, including abstract art, what do you suppose was Curry's appeal? Who do you think particularly liked Curry's pictures?

_____

_____

11. Does this picture tell a story? If so, what is it?

_____

_____

_____

12. Do you like the picture? Why or why not?

_____

_____

How the Artist Tells a Story: Homer

Winslow Homer. *"The Life Line."* 1884.

This is an etching made by the American artist Winslow Homer in 1884. It depicts a shipwrecked woman being rescued by rope and pulley. Homer devoted many paintings to subjects showing human survival against violent nature. Many of his works were set in his native New England, where high seas and fearsome storms threatened fishermen, sailors, and others who went to sea. The natural drama of these situations was heightened by Homer's style and composition.

1. What do you think is happening in this picture?

_____

_____

2. An etching is a kind of graphic art, in which the design is scratched onto the surface of a metal plate before printing. How do you think the artist used his medium (etching) to add to the drama of the picture? (Clue: Notice the waves.)

_____

_____

3. How do the strong darks and lights add to the excitement? (Clue: Try to identify what is shown as light and what is shown as dark.)

_____

_____

4. What is the source of light?

_____

5. The lines of the pulley are important both to the story and the design. How do these lines contrast with the waves and the two bodies?

_____

_____

6. In the following diagram, draw arrows to show the major directional lines of the pulley and ropes, the outline of the bodies, the waves, and the sky.

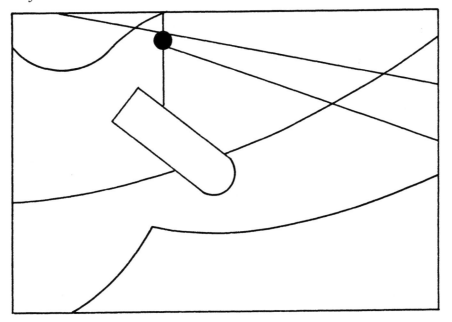

7. Where do you think the artist or viewer is standing to see this event? Near or far? Above or below? How does this point of view help convey the sense of drama?

_____

_____

8. How would including the shore, rescue boat, or the shipwreck change the picture? Would it be more or less dramatic? More or less interesting to you?

_____

_____

_____

_____

9. Why do you think this picture might be called "romantic"? Would you agree with that description?

_____

_____

_____

10. What particular parts of the two bodies emphasize the drama of the situation?

_____

_____

_____

11. What points do you think the artist is trying to make about human beings and nature?

_____

_____

_____

12. *Bonus:* On another sheet of paper, write a brief story for which this picture could be the illustration.

Exercise 50

How the Artist Tells a Story: Copley

John Singleton Copley. *"Watson and the Shark."* 1778.

This painting depicts an actual event, when a young British sailor swimming in Havana harbor was attacked by a shark and lost one foot and part of his leg before finally being rescued. (Watson survived with a wooden leg, however, and lived to become a lord mayor of London.) Copley, an American artist living in England, combined authentic detail with a highly romantic style. See if you can identify some of the characteristics of Romanticism and how they relate to the truth of this incident.

1. Describe what is happening in the picture.

_____

_____

2. What details can you find that suggest what the weather was like?

_____

_____

_____

143

3. If the pale, pure body of the drowning Watson suggests goodness and helplessness, what represents the force of evil?

_____

4. Describe Watson's saviors.

_____

_____

_____

5. Romantic artists dramatized the forces of nature. What details in Copley's painting (the sky, the sea, the light) emphasize nature's more dramatic quality?

_____

_____

6. The artist used strong contrasts to make the story dramatically powerful. What contrasts can you find that suggest the struggle between Watson and the shark? (Clue: Mention the light, the rescuers, etc.)

_____

_____

7. What details accurately tell you the setting and era of the event?

_____

_____

8. Find three or four dramatic thrusts or directional lines that conflict with one another to show the violent confrontation. For example, which thrust will kill the shark? Which suggests the sweep of the waves that pull the boat away from the victim? Which seems to pull the boat from the front of the picture into the background, so that it appears to be moving away?

_____

_____

_____

9. The formal composition of the painting is important to the dramatic message. As an admirer of Renaissance design, Copley used a generally geometric form as the basis for the composition. Can you identify it? (Clue: Its topmost point is at the high end of the spear that will kill the shark.)

_____

_____

10. This event took place in Havana harbor where Watson had gone swimming. Why do you suppose Romantic artists liked exotic locales, which they carefully and accurately depicted?

_____

_____

_____

11. List all the elements that contribute to the telling of this story and its romantic flavor. (Clue: Notice, for example, that Watson's desperately reaching hand just misses one of the savior's hands.)

_____

_____

_____

12. Do you like this picture? Why or why not?

_____

_____

_____

Picture List

Exercise 1: 1. *Inca wood carving* (Peru), c. 16th century
              2. *German sculpture*, 12th century

Exercise 2: 1. *"Sennofer, a Prince of Thebes,"* Egyptian tomb painting, Eighteenth Dynasty.

Exercise 3: 1. *Greek vase painting*, 8th century B.C.

Exercise 4: 1. *"Kneeling Woman,"* Baluba sculpture sculpture, 19–20th century (Congo)

Exercise 5: 1. *"Isabel d'Aragon."* 13th century from Cosenza, Italy
              2. *"Medieval Horseman,"* bronze sculpture, 11th–12th century (Italy)
              3. *"Martyrdom of St. Margarita,"* 12th century (Spain)

Exercise 6: 1. *"The Embarkation of Helen for Cythera"* by Master of the stories of Helen, c. 1445–70 (Renaissance Italy)
              2. *"Peasant Wedding"* by Pieter Brueghel the Elder, c. 1565 (Flemish)

Exercise 7: 1. *"Giovanni Arnolfini and His Bride"* by Jan van Eyck, 1434 (Flemish)

Exercise 8: 1. *"Raftsmen Playing Cards"* by George Caleb Bingham, 1847 (USA)

Exercise 9: 1. *"Egyptian Warrior,"* Sixth Dynasty
              2. *"Discobolus (Discus Thrower)."* c. 450 B.C. by Myron (Greece)

Exercise 10: 1. *"Portrait Bust"* by Nikolaus Gerhaert, 1467 (Flemish)
               2. *Mendi sculpture*, 16th century (Africa)
               3. *"Spiral Rhythm"* by Max Weber, orig. 1915 (USA)

Exercise 11: 1. *"Family Group"* by Henry Moore, 1945–49 (England)
               2. *"La Clairière"* by Alberto Giacometti, 1950 (Italy)

Exercise 12: 1. *"The Avenue, Middelharnis"* by Meindert Hobbema, 1689 (Holland)
               2. *"View of Taormina"* by Raoul Dufy, c. 1922–23 (France)
               3. *"Young Corn"* by Grant Wood, 1931 (USA)

Exercise 13: 1. *"Ohashi Bridge and Atake in a Sudden Shower"* by Ando Hiroshige, 19th century (Japan)

Exercise 14: 1. *"The Bedroom"* by Pieter de Hooch, c. 1660 (Holland)
               2. *Scroll painting*, 17th century (Japan)

Exercise 15: 1. *"Old Man with Gloves"* by Marcantonio Bassetti, 16th–17th century (Italy)
               2. *"Dharma"* by Kim Myong-guk, 17th century (Korea)
               3. *"Portrait of the Artist's Father"* by Jacques Villon, 1924 (France)

Exercise 16: 1. *"In the Dining Room"* by Berthe Morisot, 1886 (France)

Exercise 17:   1. *Hebrew frontispiece from a Bible,* 13th century
                2. *"Cathedral"* by Roger Bissière, 1946 (France)

Exercise 18:   1. *"View of a City"* by Ambrogio Lorenzetti, 14th century (Italy)
                2. *"Pagodas on Water"* by Paul Klee, 1927 (Switzerland)
                3. *"Eiffel Tower"* by Robert Delaunay, 1924–26 (France)

Exercise 19:   1. *"The Annunciation"* by Piero della Francesca, 1452–1466 (Italy)
                2. *"Descent from the Cross"* by Giovanni di Paolo, c. 1426 (Italy)
                3. *"The Coronation of the Virgin"* by Neri di Bicci, mid-15th century (Italy)

Exercise 20:   1. *Dutch tile design,* early 17th century (Holland)
                2. *"Quince, Cabbage, Melon and Cucumber"* by Juan Sanchez Cotán, c. 1602 (Spain)

Exercise 21:   1. *"Cats on the Roof"* by Edouard Manet, 1868 (France)
                2. *"Encounter"* by M.C. Escher, 20th century (Holland)
                3. *"Bhopal"* by Victor Vasarely, 20th century (Hungary)

Exercise 22:   1. *"The Boating Party"* by Mary Cassatt, 1893–4 (USA)

Exercise 23:   1. *Embroidered dragon,* early Ch'ing Dynasty, 1644–1911 (China)
                2. *Tile dragon,* Ming Dynasty, 1368–1644 (China)
                3. *Pottery dragon,* Ch'ing Dynasty, 1644–1911 (China)

Exercise 24:   1. *"St. Mark,"* from *Gospel Book of Archbishop Ebbo of Reims,* 9th century (France)
                2. *"The Last Judgment,"* detail of the Sistine Chapel ceiling by Michelangelo, 1508–12 (Italy)
                3. *"Nude on a Red Background"* by Fernand Léger, 1927 (France)

Exercise 25:   1. *"Icon of St. George,"* 14th century (Russia)

Exercise 26:   1. *"Three Women Dyeing Cloth"* by Shigenobu, 19th century (Japan)
                2. *Acoma Indian pottery design,* 19th–20th century (New Mexico)

Exercise 27:   1. *Chinese tile,* Ming Dynasty, 1368–1644 (China)
                2. *Japanese woodblock print,* Edo era, 1603–1867
                3. *"Cataract III"* by Bridget Riley, 1967 (England)

Exercise 28:   1. *"Unstable Displacement"* by Francisco Sobrino, 1968 (Spain)
                2. *Roman mosaic,* 1st century A.D.
                3. *Op Art design*

Exercise 29:   1. *"Judith and Maidservant with the Head of Holofernes"* by Artemisia Gentileschi, c. 1625 (Italy)

Exercise 30:   1. *"Acrobat Falling"* by Everett Shinn, 1930 (USA)

Exercise 31:   1. *"Nahkt and His Wife,"* Egyptian tomb painting, Eighteenth Dynasty
                2. *"Two Sages"* by Li T'ang, 12th century (China)
                3. *"Oarsmen at Chatou"* by Pierre Auguste Renoir, 1879 (France)

Exercise 32: 1. *"Frightened Horse"* by Théodore Géricault, 19th century (France)

Exercise 33: 1. *"The Washerwomen"* by Vincent van Gogh, 1888 (Holland)
2. *"Improvisation 28 (Second Version)"* by Wassily Kandinsky, 1912 (Russia)

Exercise 34: 1. *Mosaic* from 12th century (Italy)
2. *Bronze portrait head* from Ife, Nigeria, 12th century
3. *"Black Head"* by Pablo Picasso, 20th century (Spain)

Exercise 35: 1. *"Poor Family 2"* by Marisol (Escobar), 1987 (Venezuela)

Exercise 36: 1. *"Dam"* by Robert Rauschenberg, 1959 (USA)
2. *"The Intimacy of Water"* by Romare Bearden, 1973 (USA)

Exercise 37: 1. *"The Bullfight"* by Pablo Picasso, 1934 (Spain)
2. *"Girl Running on a Balcony"* by Giacomo Balla, 1912 (Italy)
3. *"Runners"* by Jacob Lawrence, 1972 (USA)

Exercise 38: 1. *"Father Sky and Mother Earth,"* Navajo sand painting, 20th century (Arizona)

Exercise 39: 1. *"The Five Senses"* by Baugin, c. 1630 (France)

Exercise 40: 1. *"The Eve of St. Nicholas"* by Jan Steen, c. 1660–65 (Holland)
2. *"Thanksgiving"* by Doris Lee, 1935 (USA)

Exercise 41: 1. *"Death and the Miser"* by Hieronymus Bosch, c. 1490 (Flemish)

Exercise 42: 1. *"Eviction"* by George Grosz, 1935 (Germany)
2. *"Self-Portrait"* by David Alfaro Siqueiros, 1943 (Mexico)

Exercise 43: 1. *"The Chamber of Genius"* by Thomas Rowlandson, 1812 (England)

Exercise 44: 1. *"Soft Pay-Telephone"* by Claes Oldenburg, 1963 (USA)
2. *"Dollar Sign"* by Andy Warhol, 1980 (USA)

Exercise 45: 1. *"The Nightmare"* by John Henry Fuseli, 1785–90 (Switzerland)
2. *"The Therapeutist"* by René Magritte, 1967 (Belgium)

Exercise 46: 1. *"John Brown Going to His Hanging"* by Horace Pippin, 1942 (USA)

Exercise 47: 1. *"The Blind Leading the Blind"* by Pieter Brueghel the Elder, 1568 (Flemish)

Exercise 48: 1. *"Tornado Over Kansas"* by John Steuart Curry, 1929 (USA)

Exercise 49: 1. *"The Life Line"* by Winslow Homer, 1884 (USA)

Exercise 50: 1. *"Watson and the Shark"* by John Singleton Copley, 1778 (USA)

Picture Credits

Exercise 1:   1. New York Public Library Picture Collection
                2. Bremen Cathedral, Germany

Exercise 2:   1. Egyptian Information Agency

Exercise 3:   1. New York Public Library Picture Collection

Exercise 4:   1. Royal Museum of Central Africa, Tervueren, Belgium

Exercise 5:   1. New York Public Library Picture Collection
                2. Musée du Louvre
                3. Museo Episcopal, Barcelona

Exercise 6:   1. Courtesy of The Walters Art Gallery, Baltimore
                2. Kunsthistorische Museum, Vienna

Exercise 7:   1. National Gallery, London

Exercise 8:   1. The Saint Louis Art Museum

Exercise 9:   1. Egyptian Information Agency
                2. Museo delle Terme

Exercise 10: 1. Frauenhaus, Strasbourg
                2. Private Collection
                3. Hirshhorn Museum and Sculpture Garden, Smithsonian Institution; gift of Joseph H. Hirshhorn, 1966

Exercise 11: 1. Private Collection
                2. Private Collection

Exercise 12: 1. National Gallery, London
                2. Private Collection
                3. Courtesy of Cedar Rapids, Iowa, Community School District

Exercise 13: 1. New York Public Library Picture Collection

Exercise 14: 1. National Gallery of Art, Washington; Widener Collection
                2. Courtesy of the Mary and Jackson Burke Collection

Exercise 15: 1. Museo di Castelvecchio, Verona
                2. New York Public Library Picture Collection
                3. Solomon R. Guggenheim Museum, photo by Robert E. Mates

Exercise 16: 1. National Gallery of Art, Washington; Chester Dale Collection

Exercise 17: 1. Private Collection
                2. Private Collection

Exercise 18: 1. Academia di Belle Arti, Siena
                2. Solomon R. Guggenheim Museum; photo by Myles Aronowitz
                3. Hirshhorn Museum and Sculpture Garden, Smithsonian Institution; gift of Joseph H. Hirshhorn Foundation, 1972

Exercise 19:   1. San Francesco, Arezzo
2. Courtesy of The Walters Art Gallery, Baltimore
3. Courtesy of The Walters Art Gallery, Baltimore

Exercise 20:   1. New York Public Library Picture Collection
2. San Diego Museum of Art

Exercise 21:   1. New York Public Library Picture Collection
2. Private Collection
3. Liege Museum, Belgium

Exercise 22:   1. National Gallery of Art, Washington; Chester Dale Collection

Exercise 23:   1. New York Public Library Picture Collection
2. Beijing Slide Studio, China
3. Beijing Slide Studio, China

Exercise 24:   1. Bibliothèque d'Epernay, France
2. Sistine Chapel, Rome
3. Hirshhorn Museum and Sculpture Garden, Smithsonian Institution; Gift of Joseph H. Hirshhorn Foundation, 1972

Exercise 25:   1. Leningrad Museum, USSR

Exercise 26:   1. New York Public Library Picture Collection
2. New York Public Library Picture Collection

Exercise 27:   1. Beijing Slide Studio, China
2. New York Public Library Picture Collection
3. Collection, British Council

Exercise 28:   1. Hirshhorn Museum and Sculpture Garden, Smithsonian Institution; gift of Joseph H. Hirshhorn, 1972
2. Museo delle Terme, Rome
3. New York Public Library Picture Collection

Exercise 29:   1. The Detroit Institute of Arts; Gift of Mr. Leslie H. Green

Exercise 30:   1. Hirshhorn Museum and Sculpture Garden, Smithsonian Institution

Exercise 31:   1. Egyptian Information Agency
2. Private Collection
3. National Gallery of Art, Washington; Gift of Sam A. Lewisohn, 1951

Exercise 32:   1. The Detroit Institute of Arts, gift of Mrs. James E. Scripps

Exercise 33:   1. Rijksmuseum Krollermuller, Otterlo, Holland
2. Solomon R. Guggenheim Museum, New York; photo by Robert E. Mates

Exercise 34:   1. Provincial Museum, Torcello
2. Private Collection
3. Private Collection

Exercise 35:   1. Private Collection

Exercise 36:   1. Hirshhorn Museum and Sculpture Garden, Smithsonian Institution
2. The Saint Louis Art Museum

Exercise 37: 1. The Saint Louis Art Museum
2. Civica Galleria d'Arte, Milan
3. The Seattle Art Museum, purchased with funds from PONCHO, 79.31

Exercise 38: 1. Arizona State Museum, University of Arizona

Exercise 39: 1. Musée du Louvre

Exercise 40: 1. Rijksmuseum, Amsterdam
2. The Art Institute of Chicago

Exercise 41: 1. National Gallery of Art, Washington; Samuel K. Kress Collection

Exercise 42: 1. New York Public Library Picture Collection
2. Museo de Arte Moderno, Mexico City

Exercise 43: 1. New York Public Library Picture Collection

Exercise 44: 1. Solomon R. Guggenheim Museum; photo by Robert E. Mates
2. The Forbes Collection, New York; photo by Otto E. Netson

Exercise 45: 1. Goethe Museum, Frankfurt
2. Hirshhorn Museum and Sculpture Garden, Smithsonian Institution; gift of Joseph H. Hirshhorn Foundation, 1972

Exercise 46: 1. Courtesy of the Pennsylvania Academy of the Fine Arts, Philadelphia

Exercise 47: 1. Museo Nazionale Capodimonte, Naples

Exercise 48: 1. Courtesy of the Muskegon Museum of Art, Muskegon, Michigan

Exercise 49: 1. New York Public Library Picture Collection

Exercise 50: 1. National Gallery of Art, Washington; Ferdinand Lammot Belin Fund